AF303969

Marx Hardy Machiavelli Chesterton Austen
Defoe Abbott Cooper Emerson Hugo Joyce Grimm
Melville Montaigne Haggard Eliot
Stoker Christie Molière
Wilde Carroll Maupassant Byron Schiller
Garnett Fitzgerald Engels Smith Kafka
Goethe Einstein Hawthorne Hall
Cotton Dostoyevsky Kipling Doyle Willis
Baum Henry Nietzsche
Leslie Dumas Flaubert Turgenev Balzac
Stockton Vatsyayana Crane
Burroughs Verne
Curtis Tocqueville Gogol Vinci
Homer Widger Tolstoy Whitman Busch
Darwin Thoreau Twain
Potter Freud Zola Lawrence Scott Plato Harte
Kant Jowett Stevenson Dickens Burton Hesse
Andersen
London Descartes Cervantes
Poe Aristotle Voltaire Cooke
Hale James Hastings
Bunner Shakespeare Irving
Richter Chambers da Shaw
Doré Chekhov Benedict Alcott
Dante Pushkin
Swift Wodehouse Newton

tredition®

tredition was established in 2006 by Sandra Latusseck and Soenke Schulz. Based in Hamburg, Germany, tredition offers publishing solutions to authors and publishing houses, combined with worldwide distribution of printed and digital book content. tredition is uniquely positioned to enable authors and publishing houses to create books on their own terms and without conventional manufacturing risks.

For more information please visit: www.tredition.com

TREDITION CLASSICS

This book is part of the TREDITION CLASSICS series. The creators of this series are united by passion for literature and driven by the intention of making all public domain books available in printed format again - worldwide. Most TREDITION CLASSICS titles have been out of print and off the bookstore shelves for decades. At tredition we believe that a great book never goes out of style and that its value is eternal. Several mostly non-profit literature projects provide content to tredition. To support their good work, tredition donates a portion of the proceeds from each sold copy. As a reader of a TREDITION CLASSICS book, you support our mission to save many of the amazing works of world literature from oblivion. See all available books at www.tredition.com.

 Project Gutenberg

The content for this book has been graciously provided by Project Gutenberg. Project Gutenberg is a non-profit organization founded by Michael Hart in 1971 at the University of Illinois. The mission of Project Gutenberg is simple: To encourage the creation and distribution of eBooks. Project Gutenberg is the first and largest collection of public domain eBooks.

A Voyage to Abyssinia

Jeronimo Lobo

Imprint

This book is part of TREDITION CLASSICS

Author: Jeronimo Lobo
Cover design: Buchgut, Berlin – Germany

Publisher: tredition GmbH, Hamburg - Germany
ISBN: 978-3-8424-3974-0

www.tredition.com
www.tredition.de

A VOYAGE TO ABYSSINIA.

by
FATHER JEROME LOBO.

Translated from the French
by
SAMUEL JOHNSON.

CASSELL & COMPANY, Limited:
london, paris, new york & melbourne.
1887.

INTRODUCTION.

Jeronimo Lobo was born in Lisbon in the year 1593. He entered the Order of the Jesuits at the age of sixteen. After passing through the studies by which Jesuits were trained for missionary work, which included special attention to the arts of speaking and writing, Father Lobo was sent as a missionary to India at the age of twenty-eight, in the year 1621. He reached Goa, as his book tells, in 1622, and was in 1624, at the age of thirty-one, told off as one of the missionaries to be employed in the conversion of the Abyssinians. They were to be converted, from a form of Christianity peculiar to themselves, to orthodox Catholicism. The Abyssinian Emperor Segued was protector of the enterprise, of which we have here the story told.

Father Lobo was nine years in Abyssinia, from the age of thirty-one to the age of forty, and this was the adventurous time of his life. The death of the Emperor Segued put an end to the protection that had given the devoted missionaries, in the midst of dangers, a precarious hold upon their work. When he and his comrades fell into the hands of the Turks at Massowah, his vigour of body and mind, his readiness of resource, and his fidelity, marked him out as the one to be sent to the headquarters in India to secure the payment of a ransom for his companions. He obtained the ransom, and desired also to obtain from the Portuguese Viceroy in India armed force to maintain the missionaries in the position they had so far won. But the Civil power was deaf to his pleading. He removed the appeal to Lisbon, and after narrowly escaping on the way from a shipwreck, and after having been captured by pirates, he reached Lisbon, and sought still to obtain means of overawing the force hostile to the work of the Jesuits in Abyssinia. The Princess Margaret gave friendly hearing, but sent him on to persuade, if he could, the King of Spain; and failing at Madrid, he went to Rome and tried the Pope. He was chosen to go to the Pope, said the Patriarch Alfonso Mendez, because, of all the brethren at Goa, the 'Pater Hieronymus Lupus' (Lobo translated into Wolf) was the most ingenious and learned in all sciences, with a mind most generous in its desire to conquer difficulties, dexterous in management of business, and found most able to make himself agreeable to those with whom there was business to be done. The vigour with which he held by his purpose of endeavouring in every possible way to bring the Christianity of Abyssinia within the pale of the Catholic Church is in accordance with the character that makes the centre of the story of this book. Whimsical touches arise out of this strength of character and readiness of resource, as when he tells of the taste of the Abyssinians for raw cow's flesh, with a sauce high in royal Abyssinian favour, made of the cow's gall and contents of its entrails, of which, when he was pressed to partake, he could only excuse himself and his brethren by suggesting that it was too good for such humble missionaries. Out of distinguished respect for it, they refrained from putting it into their mouths.

Good Father Lobo gave up the desire of his heart, when it was proved unattainable, and returned to India six years after the breaking up of his work in Abyssinia, at the age of forty-seven. He came to be head of the Provincials of the Jesuit settlement at Goa, and after about ten more years of active duty in the East returned in 1658 to Lisbon, when he died in the religious house of St. Roque in 1678, at the age of eighty-five. A comrade of Father Lobo's, Baltazar Tellez, said that Lobo had travelled thirty-eight thousand leagues with no other object before him but the winning of more souls to God. His years in Abyssinia stood out prominently to his mind among all the years of his long life, and he wrote an account of them in Portuguese, of which the manuscript is at Lisbon in the monastery of St. Roque, where he closed his life.

Of that manuscript, then and still unprinted (though use was made of it by Baltazar Tellez in his History of 'Ethiopia-Coimbra,' 1660), the Abbe Legrand, Prior of Neuville-les-Dames, and of Prevessin, published a translation into French. The Abbe Legrand had been to Lisbon as Secretary to the Abbe d'Estrees, Ambassador from France to Portugal. The negotiations were so long continued that M. Legrand was detained five years in Lisbon, and employed the time in researches among documents illustrating the Portuguese possessions in India and the East. He obtained many memoirs of great interest, and published from one of them an account of Ceylon; but of all the manuscripts he found none interested him so much as that of Father Lobo. His translation was augmented with illustrative dissertations, letters, and a memoir on the circumstances of the death of M. du Roule. It filled two volumes, or 636 pages of forty lines. This was published in 1728. It was on the 31st of October, 1728, that Samuel Johnson, aged nineteen, went to Pembroke College, Oxford, and Legrand's 'Voyage Historique d'Abissinie du R. P. Jerome Lobo, de la Compagnie de Jesus, Traduit du Portugais, continue et augmente de plusieurs Dissertations, Lettres et Memoires,' was one of the new books read by Johnson during his short period of college life. In 1735, when Johnson's age was twenty-six, and the world seemed to have shut against him every door of hope, Johnson stayed for six months at Birmingham with his old schoolfellow Hector, who was aiming at medical practice, and who lodged at the house of a bookseller. Johnson spoke with interest of Father Lobo, whose book he had read at Pembroke College. Mr. Warren, the bookseller, thought it would be worth while to print a translation. Hector joined in urging Johnson to undertake it, for a payment of five guineas. Although nearly brought to a stop midway by hypochondriac despondency, a little suggestion that the printers also were stopped, and if they had not their work had not their pay, caused Johnson to go on to the end. Legrand's book was reduced to a fifth of its size by the omission of all that overlaid Father Lobo's personal account of his adventures; and Johnson began work as a writer with this translation, first published at Birmingham in 1735.

H.M.

THE PREFACE

The following relation is so curious and entertaining, and the dissertations that accompany it so judicious and instructive, that the translator is confident his attempt stands in need of no apology, whatever censures may fall on the performance.

The Portuguese traveller, contrary to the general vein of his countrymen, has amused his reader with no romantic absurdities or incredible fictions; whatever he relates, whether true or not, is at least probable; and he who tells nothing exceeding the bounds of probability has a right to demand that they should believe him who cannot contradict him.

He appears by his modest and unaffected narration to have described things as he saw them, to have copied nature from the life, and to have consulted his senses, not his imagination; he meets with no basilisks that destroy with their eyes, his crocodiles devour their prey without tears, and his cataracts fall from the rock without deafening the neighbouring inhabitants.

The reader will here find no regions cursed with irremediable barrenness, or blessed with spontaneous fecundity, no perpetual gloom or unceasing sunshine; nor are the nations here described either devoid of all sense of humanity, or consummate in all private and social virtues; here are no Hottentots without religion, polity, or articulate language, no Chinese perfectly polite, and completely skilled in all sciences: he will discover, what will always be discovered by a diligent and impartial inquirer, that wherever human nature is to be found there is a mixture of vice and virtue, a contest of passion and reason, and that the Creator doth not appear partial in his distributions, but has balanced in most countries their particular inconveniences by particular favours.

In his account of the mission, where his veracity is most to be suspected, he neither exaggerates overmuch the merits of the Jesuits, if we consider the partial regard paid by the Portuguese to their countrymen, by the Jesuits to their society, and by the Papists to their church, nor aggravates the vices of the Abyssins; but if the reader will not be satisfied with a Popish account of a Popish mission, he may have recourse to the history of the church of Abyssinia, written by Dr. Geddes, in which he will find the actions and sufferings of the missionaries placed in a different light, though the same in which Mr. Le Grand, with all his zeal for the Roman church, appears to have seen them.

This learned dissertator, however valuable for his industry and erudition, is yet more to be esteemed for having dared so freely in the midst of France to declare his disapprobation of the Patriarch Oviedo's sanguinary zeal, who was continually importuning the Portuguese to beat up their drums for missionaries, who might preach the gospel with swords in their hands, and propagate by desolation and slaughter the true worship of the God of Peace.

It is not easy to forbear reflecting with how little reason these men profess themselves the followers of Jesus, who left this great characteristic to His disciples, that they should be known by loving one another, by universal and unbounded charity and benevolence.

Let us suppose an inhabitant of some remote and superior region, yet unskilled in the ways of men, having read and considered the precepts of the gospel, and the example of our Saviour, to come down in search of the true church: if he would not inquire after it among the cruel, the insolent, and the oppressive; among those who are continually grasping at dominion over souls as well as bodies; among those who are employed in procuring to themselves impunity for the most enormous villainies, and studying methods of destroying their fellow-creatures, not for their crimes but their errors; if he would not expect to meet benevolence, engage in massacres, or to find mercy in a court of inquisition, he would not look for the true church in the Church of Rome.

Mr. Le Grand has given in one dissertation an example of great moderation, in deviating from the temper of his religion, but in the others has left proofs that learning and honesty are often too weak to oppose prejudice. He has made no scruple of preferring the testimony of Father du Bernat to the writings of all the Portuguese Jesuits, to whom he allows great zeal, but little learning, without giving any other reason than that his favourite was a Frenchman. This is writing only to Frenchmen and to Papists: a Protestant would be desirous to know why he must imagine that Father du

Bernat had a cooler head or more knowledge; and why one man whose account is singular is not more likely to be mistaken than many agreeing in the same account.

If the Portuguese were biassed by any particular views, another bias equally powerful may have deflected the Frenchman from the truth, for they evidently write with contrary designs: the Portuguese, to make their mission seem more necessary, endeavoured to place in the strongest light the differences between the Abyssinian and Roman Church; but the great Ludolfus, laying hold on the advantage, reduced these later writers to prove their conformity.

Upon the whole, the controversy seems of no great importance to those who believe the Holy Scriptures sufficient to teach the way of salvation, but of whatever moment it may be thought, there are not proofs sufficient to decide it.

His discourses on indifferent subjects will divert as well as instruct, and if either in these, or in the relation of Father Lobo, any argument shall appear unconvincing, or description obscure, they are defects incident to all mankind, which, however, are not too rashly to be imputed to the authors, being sometimes, perhaps, more justly chargeable on the translator.

In this translation, if it may be so called, great liberties have been taken, which, whether justifiable or not, shall be fairly confessed; and let the judicious part of mankind pardon or condemn them.

In the first part the greatest freedom has been used in reducing the narration into a narrow compass, so that it is by no means a translation but an epitome, in which, whether everything either useful or entertaining be comprised, the compiler is least qualified to determine.

In the account of Abyssinia, and the continuation, the authors have been followed with more exactness, and as few passages appeared either insignificant or tedious, few have been either shortened or omitted.

The dissertations are the only part in which an exact translation has been attempted, and even in those abstracts are sometimes given instead of literal quotations, particularly in the first; and sometimes other parts have been contracted.

Several memorials and letters, which are printed at the end of the dissertations to secure the credit of the foregoing narrative, are entirely left out.

It is hoped that, after this confession, whoever shall compare this attempt with the original, if he shall find no proofs of fraud or partiality, will candidly overlook any failure of judgment.

PART I – THE VOYAGE TO ABYSSINIA

CHAPTER I

The author arrives after some difficulties at Goa. Is chosen for the Mission of Fthiopia. The fate of those Jesuits who went by Zeila. The author arrives at the coast of Melinda.

I embarked in March, 1622, in the same fleet with the Count Vidigueira, on whom the king had conferred the viceroyship of the Indies, then vacant by the resignation of Alfonso Noronha, whose unsuccessful voyage in the foregoing year had been the occasion of the loss of Ormus, which being by the miscarriage of that fleet deprived of the succours necessary for its defence, was taken by the Persians and English. The beginning of this voyage was very prosperous: we were neither annoyed with the diseases of the climate nor distressed with bad weather, till we doubled the Cape of Good Hope, which was about the end of May. Here began our misfortunes; these coasts are remarkable for the many shipwrecks the Portuguese have suffered. The sea is for the most part rough, and the winds tempestuous; we had here our rigging somewhat damaged by a storm of lightning, which when we had repaired, we sailed forward to Mosambique, where we were to stay some time. When we came near that coast, and began to rejoice at the prospect of ease and refreshment, we were on the sudden alarmed with the sight of a squadron of ships, of what nation we could not at first distinguish, but soon discovered that they were three English and three Dutch, and were preparing to attack us. I shall not trouble the reader with the particulars of this fight, in which, though the English commander ran himself aground, we lost three of our ships, and with great difficulty escaped with the rest into the port of Mosambique.

This place was able to afford us little consolation in our uneasy circumstances; the arrival of our company almost caused a scarcity of provisions. The heat in the day is intolerable, and the dews in the night so unwholesome that it is almost certain death to go out with one's head uncovered. Nothing can be a stronger proof of the malignant quality of the air than that the rust will immediately corrode both the iron and brass if they are not carefully covered with straw.

We stayed, however, in this place from the latter end of July to the beginning of September, when having provided ourselves with other vessels, we set out for Cochim, and landed there after a very hazardous and difficult passage, made so partly by the currents and storms which separated us from each other, and partly by continual apprehensions of the English and Dutch, who were cruising for us in the Indian seas. Here the viceroy and his company were received with so much ceremony, as was rather troublesome than pleasing to us who were fatigued with the labours of the passage; and having stayed here some time, that the gentlemen who attended the viceroy to Goa might fit out their vessels, we set sail, and after having been detained some time at sea, by calms and contrary winds, and somewhat harassed by the English and Dutch, who were now increased to eleven ships of war, arrived at Goa, on Saturday, the 16th of December, and the viceroy made his entry with great magnificence.

I lived here about a year, and completed my studies in divinity; in which time some letters were received from the fathers in Fthiopia, with an account that Sultan Segued, Emperor of Abyssinia, was converted to the Church of Rome, that many of his subjects had followed his example, and that there was a great want of missionaries to improve these prosperous beginnings. Everybody was very desirous of seconding the zeal of our fathers, and of sending them the assistance they requested; to which we were the more encouraged, because the emperor's letters informed our provincial that we might easily enter his dominions by the way of Dancala, but unhappily, the secretary wrote Zeila for Dancala, which cost two of our fathers their lives.

We were, however, notwithstanding the assurances given us by the emperor, sufficiently apprised of the danger which we were exposed to in this expedition, whether we went by sea or land. By sea, we foresaw the hazard we run of falling into the hands of the Turks, amongst whom we should lose, if not our lives, at least our liberty, and be for ever prevented from reaching the court of Fthiopia. Upon this consideration our superiors divided the eight Jesuits chosen for this mission into two companies. Four they sent by sea and four by land; I was of the latter number. The four first were the more fortunate, who though they were detained some time by the

Turkish bassa, were dismissed at the request of the emperor, who sent him a zebra, or wild ass, a creature of large size and admirable beauty.

As for us, who were to go by Zeila, we had still greater difficulties to struggle with: we were entirely strangers to the ways we were to take, to the manners, and even to the names of the nations through which we were to pass. Our chief desire was to discover some new road by which we might avoid having anything to do with the Turks. Among great numbers whom we consulted on this occasion, we were informed by some that we might go through Melinda. These men painted that hideous wilderness in charming colours, told us that we should find a country watered with navigable rivers, and inhabited by a people that would either inform us of the way, or accompany us in it. These reports charmed us, because they flattered our desires; but our superiors finding nothing in all this talk that could be depended on, were in suspense what directions to give us, till my companion and I upon this reflection, that since all the ways were equally new to us, we had nothing to do but to resign ourselves to the Providence of God, asked and obtained the permission of our superiors to attempt the road through Melinda. So of we who went by land, two took the way of Zeila, and my companion and I that of Melinda.

Those who were appointed for Zeila embarked in a vessel that was going to Caxume, where they were well received by the king, and accommodated with a ship to carry them to Zeila; they were there treated by the check with the same civility which they had met with at Caxume. But the king being informed of their arrival, ordered them to be conveyed to his court at Auxa, to which place they were scarce come before they were thrown by the king's command into a dark and dismal dungeon, where there is hardly any sort of cruelty that was not exercised upon them. The Emperor of Abyssinia endeavoured by large offers to obtain their liberty, but his kind offices had no other effect than to heighten the rage of the king of Zeila. This prince, besides his ill will to Sultan Segued, which was kept up by some malcontents among the Abyssin nobility, who, provoked at the conversion of their master, were plotting a revolt, entertained an inveterate hatred against the Portuguese for the death of his grandfather, who had been killed many years before, which he swore the blood of the Jesuits should repay. So after they had languished for some time in prison their heads were struck off. A fate which had been likewise our own, had not God reserved us for longer labours!

Having provided everything necessary for our journey, such as Arabian habits, and red caps, calicoes, and other trifles to make presents of to the inhabitants, and taking leave of our friends, as men going to a speedy death, for we were not insensible of the dangers we were likely to encounter, amongst horrid deserts, impassable mountains, and barbarous nations, we left Goa on the 26th day of January in the year 1624, in a Portuguese galliot that was ordered to set us ashore at Pate, where we landed without any disaster in eleven days, together with a young Abyssin, whom we made use of as our interpreter. While we stayed here we were given to understand that those who had been pleased at Goa to give us directions in relation to our journey had done nothing but tell us lies. That the people were savage, that they had indeed begun to treat with the Portuguese, but it was only from fear, that otherwise they were a barbarous nation, who finding themselves too much crowded in their own country, had extended themselves to the sea-shore; that they ravished the country and laid everything waste where they came, that they were man-eaters, and were on that account dreadful in all those parts. My companion and I being undeceived by this terrible relation, thought it would be the highest imprudence to expose ourselves both together to a death almost certain and unprofitable, and agreed that I should go with our Abyssin and a Portuguese to observe the country; that if I should prove so happy as to escape being killed by the inhabitants, and to discover a way, I should either return, or send back the Abyssin or Portuguese. Having fixed upon this, I hired a little bark to Jubo, a place about forty leagues distant from Pate, on board which I put some provisions, together with my sacerdotal vestments, and all that was necessary for saying mass: in this vessel we reached the coast, which we found inhabited by several nations: each nation is subject to its own king; these petty monarchies are so numerous, that I counted at least ten in less than four leagues.

CHAPTER II

The author lands: The difficulty of his journey. An account of the Galles, and of the author's reception at the king's tent; Their manner of swearing, and of letting blood. The author returns to the Indies, and finds the patriarch of Fthiopia.

On this coast we landed, with an intention of travelling on foot to Jubo, a journey of much greater length and difficulty than we imagined. We durst not go far from our bark, and therefore were obliged to a toilsome march along the windings of the shore, sometimes clambering up rocks, and sometimes wading through the sands, so that we were every moment in the utmost danger of falling from the one, or sinking in the other. Our lodging was either in the rocks or on the sands, and even that incommoded by continual apprehensions of being devoured by lions and tigers. Amidst all these calamities our provisions failed us; we had little hopes of a supply, for we found neither villages, houses, nor any trace of a human creature; and had miserably perished by thirst and hunger had we not met with some fishermen's boats, who exchanged their fish for tobacco.

Through all these fatigues we at length came to Jubo, a kingdom of considerable extent, situated almost under the line, and tributary to the Portuguese, who carry on a trade here for ivory and other commodities. This region so abounds with elephants, that though the teeth of the male only are valuable, they load several ships with ivory every year. All this coast is much infested with ravenous beasts, monkeys, and serpents, of which last here are some seven feet in length, and thicker than an ordinary man; in the head of this serpent is found a stone about the bigness of an egg, resembling bezoar, and of great efficacy, as it is said, against all kinds of poison. I stayed here some time to inform myself whether I might, by pursuing this road, reach Abyssinia; and could get no other intelligence but that two thousand Galles (the same people who inhabited Melinda) had encamped about three leagues from Jubo; that they had been induced to fix in that place by the plenty of provisions they found there. These Galles lay everything where they come in ruin, putting all to the sword without distinction of age or sex; which barbarities, though their numbers are not great, have spread the terror of them over all the country. They choose a king, whom they call Lubo: every eighth year they carry their wives with them, and expose their children without any tenderness in the woods, it being prohibited, on pain of death, to take any care of those which are born in the camp. This is their way of living when they are in arms, but afterwards when they settle at home they breed up their children. They feed upon raw cow's flesh; when they kill a cow, they keep the blood to rub their bodies with, and wear the guts about their necks for ornaments, which they afterwards give to their wives.

Several of these Galles came to see me, and as it seemed they had never beheld a white man before, they gazed on me with amazement; so strong was their curiosity that they even pulled off my shoes and stockings, that they might be satisfied whether all my body was of the same colour with my face. I could remark, that after they had observed me some time, they discovered some aversion from a white; however, seeing me pull out my handkerchief, they asked me for it with a great deal of eagerness; I cut it into several pieces that I might satisfy them all, and distributed it amongst them; they bound them about their heads, but gave me to understand that they should have liked them better if they had been red: after this we were seldom without their company, which gave occasion to an accident, which though it seemed to threaten some danger at first, turned afterwards to our advantage.

As these people were continually teasing us, our Portuguese one day threatened in jest to kill one of them. The black ran in the utmost dread to seek his comrades, and we were in one moment almost covered with Galles; we thought it the most proper course to decline the first impulse of their fury, and retired into our house. Our retreat inspired them with courage; they redoubled their cries, and posted themselves on an eminence near at hand that overlooked us; there they insulted us by brandishing their lances and daggers. We were fortunately not above a stone's cast from the sea, and could therefore have retreated to our bark had we found ourselves reduced to extremities. This made us not very solicitous about their menaces; but finding that they continued to hover about our habitation, and being wearied with their clamours, we thought it might be a good expedient to fright them away by firing four muskets towards them, in such a manner that they might hear the bullets hiss about two feet over their heads. This had the effect we wished; the noise and fire of our arms struck them with so much terror that they fell upon the ground, and durst not for some time so much as lift up their heads. They forgot immediately their natural temper, their ferocity and haughtiness were softened into mildness and submission; they asked pardon for their insolence, and we were ever after good friends.

After our reconciliation we visited each other frequently, and had some conversation about the journey I had undertaken, and the desire I had of finding a new passage into Fthiopia. It was necessary on this account to consult their lubo or king: I found him in a straw hut something larger than those of his subjects, surrounded by his courtiers, who had each a stick in his hand, which is longer or shorter according to the quality of the person admitted into the king's presence. The ceremony made use of at the reception of a stranger is somewhat unusual; as soon as he enters, all the courtiers strike him with their cudgels till he goes back to the door; the amity then subsisting between us did not secure me from this uncouth reception, which they told me, upon my demanding the reason of it, was to show those whom they treated with that they were the bravest people in the world, and that all other nations ought to bow down before them. I could not help reflecting on this occasion how imprudently I had trusted my life in the hands of men unacquainted with compassion of civility, but recollecting at the same time that the intent of my journey was such as might give me hopes of the divine protection, I banished all thoughts but those of finding a way into Fthiopia. In this strait it occurred to me that these people, however barbarous, have some oath which they keep with an inviolable strictness; the best precaution, therefore, that I could use would be to bind them by this oath to be true to their engagements. The manner of their swearing is this: they set a sheep in the midst of them, and rub it over with butter, the heads of families who are the chief in the nation lay their hands upon the head of the sheep, and swear to observe their promise. This oath (which they never violate) they explain thus: the sheep is the mother of them who swear; the butter betokens the love between the mother and the children, and an oath taken on a mother's head is sacred. Upon the security of this oath, I made them acquainted with my intention, an intention, they told me, it was impossible to put in execution. From the moment I left them they said they could give me no assurance of either life or liberty, that they were perfectly informed both of the roads and inhabitants, that there were no fewer than nine nations between us and Abyssinia, who were always embroiled amongst themselves, or at war with the Abyssins, and enjoyed no security even in their own territories. We were now convinced that our enterprise was impracticable, and that to hazard ourselves amidst so many insurmountable difficulties would be to tempt Providence; despairing, therefore, that I should ever come this way to Abyssinia, I resolved to return back with my intelligence to my companion, whom I had left at Pate.

I cannot, however, leave this country without giving an account of their manner of blood-letting, which I was led to the knowledge of by a violent fever, which threatened to put an end to my life and travels together. The distress I was in may easily be imagined, being entirely destitute of everything necessary. I had resolved to let myself blood, though I was altogether a stranger to the manner of doing it, and had no lancet, but my companions hearing of a surgeon of reputation in the place, went and brought him. I saw, with the utmost surprise, an old Moor enter my chamber, with a kind of small dagger, all over rusty, and a mallet in his hand, and three cups of horn about half a foot long. I started, and asked what he wanted. He told me to bleed me; and when I had given him leave, uncovering my side, applied one of his horn cups, which he stopped with chewed paper, and by that means made it stick fast; in the same manner he fixed on the other two, and fell to sharpening his instrument, assuring me that he would give me no pain. He then took off his cups, and gave in each place a stroke with his poignard, which was followed by a stream of blood. He applied his cups several times, and every time struck his lancet into the same place; having drawn away a large quantity of blood, he healed the orifices with three lumps of tallow. I know not whether to attribute my cure to bleeding or my fear, but I had from that time no return of my fever.

When I came to Pate, in hopes of meeting with my associate, I found that he was gone to Mombaza, in hopes of receiving information. He was sooner undeceived than I, and we met at the place where we parted in a few days; and soon afterwards left Pate to return to the Indies, and in nine-and-twenty days arrived at the famous fortress of Diou. We were told at this place that Alfonso Mendes, patriarch of Fthiopia, was arrived at Goa from Lisbon. He wrote to us to desire that we would wait for him at Diou, in order to embark there for the Red Sea; but being informed by us that no opportunities of going thither were to be expected at Diou, it was at length determined that we should meet at Bazaim; it was no easy matter for me to find means of going to Bazaim. However, after a very uneasy voyage, in which we were often in danger of being dashed against the rocks, or thrown upon the sands by the rapidity of the current, and suffered the utmost distress for want of water, I landed at Daman, a place about twenty leagues distant from Bazaim. Here I hire a catre and four boys to carry me to Bazaim: these catres are a kind of travelling couches, in which you may either lie or sit, which the boys, whose business is the same with that of chairmen in our country, support upon their shoulders by two poles, and carry a passenger at the rate of eighteen or twenty miles a day. Here we at length found the patriarch, with three more priests, like us, designed for the mission of Fthiopia. We went back to Daman, and from thence to Diou, where we arrived in a short time.

CHAPTER III

The author embarks with the patriarch, narrowly escapes shipwreck near the isle of Socotora; enters the Arabian Gulf, and the Red Sea. Some account of the coast of the Red Sea.

The patriarch having met with many obstacles and disappointments in his return to Abyssinia, grew impatient of being so long absent from his church. Lopo Gomez d'Abreu had made him an offer at Bazaim of fitting out three ships at his own expense, provided a commission could be procured him to cruise in the Red Sea. This proposal was accepted by the patriarch, and a commission granted by the viceroy. While we were at Diou, waiting for these vessels, we received advice from Fthiopia that the emperor, unwilling to expose the patriarch to any hazard, thought Dagher, a port in the mouth of the Red Sea, belonging to a prince dependent on the Abyssins, a place of the greatest security to land at, having already written to that prince to give him safe passage through his dominions. We met here with new delays; the fleet that was to transport us did not appear, the patriarch lost all patience, and his zeal so much affected the commander at Diou, that he undertook to equip a vessel for us, and pushed the work forward with the utmost diligence. At length, the long-expected ships entered the port; we were overjoyed, we were transported, and prepared to go on board. Many persons at Diou, seeing the vessels so well fitted out, desired leave to go this voyage along with us, imagining they had an excellent opportunity of acquiring both wealth and honour. We committed, however, one great error in setting out, for having equipped our ships for privateering, and taken no merchandise on board, we could not touch at any of the ports of the Red Sea. The patriarch, impatient to be gone, took leave in the most tender manner of the governor and his other friends, recommended our voyage to the Blessed Virgin, and in the field, before we went on shipboard, made a short exhortation, so moving and pathetic, that it touched the hearts of all who heard it. In the evening we went on board, and early the next morning being the 3rd of April, 1625, we set sail.

After some days we discovered about noon the island Socotora, where we proposed to touch. The sky was bright and the wind fair, nor had we the least apprehension of the danger into which we were falling, but with the utmost carelessness and jollity held on our course. At night, when our sailors, especially the Moors, were in a profound sleep (for the Mohammedans, believing everything forewritten in the decrees of God, and not alterable by any human means, resign themselves entirely to Providence), our vessel ran aground upon a sand bank at the entrance of the harbour. We got her off with the utmost difficulty, and nothing but a miracle could have preserved us. We ran along afterwards by the side of the island, but were entertained with no other prospect than of a mountainous country, and of rocks that jutted out over the sea, and seemed ready to fall into it. In the afternoon, putting into the most convenient ports of the island, we came to anchor; very much to the amazement and terror of the inhabitants, who were not used to see any Portuguese ships upon their coasts, and were therefore under a great consternation at finding them even in their ports. Some ran for security to the mountains, others took up arms to oppose our landing, but were soon reconciled to us, and brought us fowls, fish, and sheep, in exchange for India calicoes, on which they set a great value. We left this island early the next morning, and soon came in sight of Cape Gardafui, so celebrated heretofore under the name of the Cape of Spices, either because great quantities were then found there, or from its neighbourhood to Arabia the Happy, even at this day famous for its fragrant products. It is properly at this cape (the most eastern part of Africa) that the Gulf of Arabia begins, which at Babelmandel loses its name, and is called the Red Sea. Here, though the weather was calm, we found the sea so rough, that we were tossed as in a high wind for two nights; whether this violent agitation of the water proceeded from the narrowness of the strait, or from the fury of the late storm, I know not; whatever was the cause, we suffered all the hardships of a tempest. We continued our course towards the Red Sea, meeting with nothing in our passage but a gelve, or kind of boat, made of thin boards, sewed together, with no other sail than a mat. We gave her chase, in hopes of being informed by the crew whether there were any Arabian vessels at the mouth of the strait; but the Moors, who all entertain dismal apprehensions of the Franks, plied their oars and sail with the utmost diligence, and as soon as they reached land, quitted their boat, and scoured to the mountains. We saw them make signals from thence, and imagining they would come to a parley, sent out our boat with two sailors and an Abyssin, putting the ships off from the shore, to set them free from any suspicion of danger in coming down. All this was to no purpose, they could not be drawn from the mountain, and our men had orders not to go on shore, so they were obliged to return without information. Soon after we discovered the isle of Babelmandel, which gives name to the strait so called, and parts the sea that surrounds it into two channels; that on the side of Arabia is not above a quarter of a league in breadth, and through this pass almost all the vessels that trade to or from the Red Sea. The other, on the side of Fthiopia, though much larger, is more dangerous, by reason of the shallows, which make it necessary for a ship, though of no great burthen, to pass very near the island, where the channel is deeper and less embarrassed. This passage is never made use of but by those who would avoid meeting with the Turks who are stationed on the coast of Arabia; it was for this reason that we chose it. We passed it in the night, and entered that sea, so renowned on many accounts in history, both sacred and profane.

In our description of this famous sea, an account of which may justly be expected in this place, it is most convenient to begin with the coast of Arabia, on which part at twelve leagues from the mouth stands the city of Moca, a place of considerable trade. Forty leagues farther is the Isle of Camaram, whose inhabitants are annoyed with little serpents, which they call basilisks, which, though very poisonous and deadly, do not, as the ancients have told us, kill with their eyes, or if they have so fatal a power, it is not at least in this place. Sailing ninety leagues farther, you see the noted port of Jodda, where the pilgrims that go to Mecca and Medina unlade those rich presents which the zeal of different princes is every day accumulating at the tomb of Mahomet. The commerce of this place, and the number of merchants that resort thither from all parts of the world, are above description, and so richly laden are the ships that come hither, that when the Indians would express a thing of inestimable price, they say, "It is of greater value than a ship of Jodda." An hundred and eighteen leagues from thence lies Toro, and near it the ruins of an ancient monastery. This is the place, if the report of the inhabitants deserves any credit, where the Israelites miraculously passed through the Red Sea on dry land; and there is some reason for imagining the tradition not ill grounded, for the sea is here only three leagues in breadth. All the ground about Toro is barren for want of water, which is only to be found at a considerable distance, in one fountain, which flows out of the neighbouring mountains, at the foot of which there are still twelve palm-trees. Near Toro are several wells, which, as the Arabs tell us, were dug by the order of Moses to quiet the clamours of the thirsty Israelites. Suez lies in the bottom of the Gulf, three leagues from Toro, once a place of note, now reduced, under the Turks, to an inconsiderable village, where the miserable inhabitants are forced to fetch water at three leagues' distance. The ancient Kings of Egypt conveyed the waters of the Nile to this place by an artificial canal, now so choked with sand, that there are scarce any marks remaining of so noble and beneficial a work.

The first place to be met with in travelling along the coast of Africa is Rondelo, situate over against Toro, and celebrated for the same miraculous passage. Forty-five leagues from thence is Cocir. Here ends that long chain of mountains that reaches from this place even to the entrance of the Red Sea. In this prodigious ridge, which extends three hundred leagues, sometimes approaching near the sea, and sometimes running far up into the land, there is only one opening, through which all that merchandise is conveyed, which is embarked at Rifa, and from thence distributed through all the east. These mountains, as they are uncultivated, are in some parts shaded with large forests, and in others dry and bare. As they are exceedingly high, all the seasons may be here found together; when the storms of winter beat on one side, on the other is often a serene sky and a bright sunshine. The Nile runs here so near the shore that it might without much difficulty be turned through this opening of the mountains into the Red Sea, a design which many of the Emperors have thought of putting in execution, and thereby making a communication between the Red Sea and the Mediterranean, but have been discouraged either by the greatness of the expense or the fear of laying great part of Egypt under water, for some of that country lies lower than sea.

Distant from Rondelo a hundred and thirty leagues is the Isle of Suaquem, where the Bassa of that country chooses his residence, for the convenience of receiving the tribute with greater exactness, there being a large trade carried on here with the Abyssins. The Turks of Suaquem have gardens on the firm land, not above a musket shot from the island, which supply them with many excellent herbs and fruits, of which I doubt whether there be not a greater quantity on this little spot than on the whole coast of Africa besides, from Melinda to Suez. For if we except the dates which grow between Suez and Suaquem, the ground does not yield the least product; all the necessaries of life, even water, is wanting. Nothing can support itself in this region of barrenness but ostriches, which devour stones, or anything they meet with; they lay a great number of eggs, part of which they break to feed their young with. These fowls, of which I have seen many, are very tame, and when they are pursued, stretch out their wings, and run with amazing swiftness. As they have cloven feet, they sometimes strike up the stones when they run, which gave occasion to the notion that they threw stones at the hunters, a relation equally to be credited with those of their eating fire and digesting iron. Those feathers which are so much valued grow under their wings: the shell of their eggs powdered is an excellent remedy for sore eyes.

The burning wind spoken of in the sacred writings, I take to be that which the natives term arur, and the Arabs uri, which blowing in the spring, brings with it so excessive a heat, that the whole country seems a burning oven; so that there is no travelling here in this dreadful season, nor is this the only danger to which the unhappy passenger is exposed in these uncomfortable regions. There blows in the months of June, July, and August, another wind, which raises mountains of sand and carries them through the air; all that can be done in this case is when a cloud of sand rises, to mark where it is likely to fall, and to retire as far off as possible; but it is very usual for men to be taken unexpectedly, and smothered in the dust. One day I found the body of a Christian, whom I knew, upon the sand; he had doubtless been choked by these winds. I recommended his soul to the divine mercy and buried him. He seemed to have been some time dead, yet the body had no ill smell. These winds are most destructive in Arabia the Desert.

CHAPTER IV

The author's conjecture on the name of the Red Sea. An account of the cocoa-tree. He lands at Baylur.

To return to the description of the coast: sixty leagues from Suaquem is an island called Mazna, only considerable for its ports, which make the Turks reside upon it, though they are forced to keep three barks continually employed in fetching water, which is not to be found nearer than at a distance of twelve miles. Forty leagues from hence is Dalacha, an island where many pearls are found, but of small value. The next place is Baylur, forty leagues from Dalacha, and twelve from Babelmandel.

There are few things upon which a greater variety of conjectures has been offered than upon the reasons that induced the ancients to distinguish this gulf, which separates Asia from Africa, by the name of the Red Sea, an appellation that has almost universally obtained in all languages. Some affirm that the torrents, which fall after great rains from the mountains, wash down such a quantity of red sand as gives a tincture to the water: others tell us that the sunbeams being reverberated from the red rocks, give the sea on which they strike the appearance of that colour. Neither of these accounts are satisfactory; the coasts are so scorched by the heat that they are rather black than red; nor is the colour of this sea much altered by the winds or rains. The notion generally received is, that the coral found in such quantities at the bottom of the sea might communicate this colour to the water: an account merely chimerical. Coral is not to be found in all parts of this gulf, and red coral in very few. Nor does this water in fact differ from that of other seas. The patriarch and I have frequently amused ourselves with making observations, and could never discover any redness, but in the shallows, where a kind of weed grew which they call gouesmon, which redness disappeared as soon as we plucked up the plant. It is observable that St. Jerome, confining himself to the Hebrew, calls this sea Jamsuf. Jam in that language signifies sea, and suf is the name of a plant in Fthiopia, from which the Abyssins extract a beautiful crimson; whether this be the same with the gouesmon, I know not, but am of opinion that the herb gives to this sea both the colour and the name.

The vessels most used in the Red Sea, though ships of all sizes may be met with there, are gelves, of which some mention hath been made already; these are the more convenient, because they will not split if thrown upon banks or against rocks. These gelves have given occasion to the report that out of the cocoa-tree alone a ship may be built, fitted out with masts, sails, and cordage, and victualled with bread, water, wine, sugar, vinegar, and oil. All this indeed cannot be done out of one tree, but may out of several of the same kind. They saw the trunk into planks, and sew them together with thread which they spin out of the bark, and which they twist for the cables; the leaves stitched together make the sails. This boat thus equipped may be furnished with all necessaries from the same tree. There is not a month in which the cocoa does not produce a bunch of nuts, from twenty to fifty. At first sprouts out a kind of seed or capsula, of a shape not unlike the scabbard of a scimitar, which they cut, and place a vessel under, to receive the liquor that drops from it; this drink is called soro, and is clear, pleasant, and nourishing. If it be boiled, it grows hard, and makes a kind of sugar much valued in the Indies: distil this liquor and you have a strong water, of which is made excellent vinegar. All these different products are afforded before the nut is formed, and while it is green it contains a delicious cooling water; with these nuts they store their gelves, and it is the only provision of water which is made in this country. The second bark which contains the water is so tender that they eat it. When this fruit arrives to perfect maturity, they either pound the kernel into meal, and make cakes of or draw an oil from it of a fine scent and taste, and of great use in medicine; so that what is reported of the different products of this wonderful tree is neither false nor incredible.

It is time we should come now to the relation of our voyage. Having happily passed the straits at the entrance of the Red Sea, we pursued our course, keeping as near the shore as we could, without any farther apprehensions of the Turks. We were, however, under some concern that we were entirely ignorant in what part of the coast to find Baylur, a port where we proposed landing, and so little known, that our pilots, who had made many voyages in this sea, could give us no account of it. We were in hopes of information from the fishermen, but found that as soon as we came near they fled from us in the greatest consternation; no signals of peace or friendship could prevail on them to stay; they either durst not trust or did not understand us. We plied along the coast in this uncertainty two days, till on the first of March having doubled a point of land, which came out a great way into the sea, we found ourselves in the middle of a fair large bay, which many reasons induced us to think was Baylur; that we might be farther assured we sent our Abyssin on shore, who returning next morning confirmed our opinion. It would not be easy to determine whether our arrival gave us greater joy, or the inhabitants greater apprehensions, for we could discern a continual tumult in the land, and took notice that the crews of some barks that lay in the harbour were unlading with all possible diligence, to prevent the cargo from falling into our hands, very much indeed to the dissatisfaction of many of our soldiers, who having engaged in this expedition, with no other view than of filling their pockets, were, before the return of our Abyssin, for treating them like enemies, and taking them as a lawful prize. We were willing to be assured of a good reception in this port; the patriarch therefore sent me to treat with them. I dressed myself like a merchant, and in that habit received the four captains of gelves which the chec sent to compliment me, and ordered to stay as hostages, whom I sent back, that I might gain upon their affections by the confidence I placed in their sincerity; this had so good an effect, that the chec, who was transported with the account the officers gave of the civilities they had been treated with, came in an hour to visit me, bringing with him a Portuguese, whom I had sent ashore as a security for his return. He informed me that the King his master was encamped not far off, and that a chec who was then in the company was just arrived from thence, and had seen the Emperor of Fthiopia's letters in our favour; I was then convinced that we might land without scruple, and to give the patriarch notice of it ordered a volley of our muskets to be fired, which was answered by the cannon of the two ships that lay at a distance, for fear of giving the Moors any cause of suspicion by their approach. The chec and his attendants, though I had given them notice that we were going to let off our guns in honour of the King their master, could not forbear trembling at the fire and noise. They left us soon after, and next morning we landed our baggage, consisting chiefly of the patriarch's library, some ornaments for the church, some images, and some pieces of calico, which were of the same use as money. Most of the soldiers and sailors were desirous of going with us, some from real principles of piety, and a desire of sharing the labours and merits of the mission, others upon motives very different, the hopes of raising a fortune. To have taken all who offered themselves would have been an injury to the owners of the ships, by rendering them unable to continue their voyage; we therefore accepted only of a few.

CHAPTER V

An account of Dancali. The conduct of Chec Furt. The author wounded. They arrive at the court of the King of Dancali. A description of his pavilion, and the reception they met with.

Our goods were no sooner landed than we were surrounded with a crowd of officers, all gaping for presents; we were forced to gratify their avarice by opening our bales, and distributing among them some pieces of calico. What we gave to the chec might be worth about a pistole, and the rest in proportion.

The kingdom of Dancali, to which this belongs, is barren, and thinly peopled; the king is tributary to the Emperor of Abyssinia, and very faithful to his sovereign. The emperor had not only written to him, but had sent a Moor and Portuguese as his ambassadors, to secure us a kind reception; these in their way to this prince had come through the countries of Chumo-Salamay and Senaa, the utmost confines of Abyssinia, and had carried thither the emperor's orders concerning our passage.

On Ascension Day we left Baylur, having procured some camels and asses to carry our baggage. The first day's march was not above a league, and the others not much longer. Our guides performed their office very ill, being influenced, as we imagined, by the Chec Furt, an officer, whom, though unwilling, we were forced to take with us. This man, who might have brought us to the king in three days, led us out of the way through horrid deserts destitute of water, or where what we found was so foul, nauseous, and offensive, that it excited a loathing and aversion which nothing but extreme necessity could have overcome.

Having travelled some days, we were met by the King's brother, to whom, by the advice of Chec Furt, whose intent in following us was to squeeze all he could from us; we presented some pieces of Chinese workmanship, such as cases of boxes, a standish, and some earthenware, together with several pieces of painted calico, which were so much more agreeable, that he desired some other pieces instead of our Chinese curiosities; we willingly made the exchange. Yet some time afterwards he asked again for those Chinese goods which he had returned us, nor was it in our power to refuse them. I was here in danger of losing my life by a compliment which the Portuguese paid the prince of a discharge of twelve muskets; one being unskilfully charged too high, flew out of the soldier's hand, and falling against my leg, wounded it very much; we had no surgeon with us, so that all I could do was to bind it hard with some cloth. I was obliged by this accident to make use of the Chec Furt's horse, which was the greatest service we received from him in all our journey.

When we came within two leagues and a half of the King's court, he sent some messengers with his compliments, and five mules for the chief of our company. Our road lay through a wood, where we found the ground covered over with young locusts, a plague intolerably afflictive in a country so barren of itself. We arrived at length at the bank of a small river, near which the King usually keeps his residence, and found his palace at the foot of a little mountain. It consisted of about six tents and twenty cabins, erected amongst some thorns and wild trees, which afforded a shelter from the heat of the weather. He received us the first time in a cabin about a musket shot distant from the rest, furnished out with a throne in the middle built of clay and stones, and covered with tapestry and two velvet cushions. Over against him stood his horse with his saddle and other furniture hanging by him, for in this country, the master and his horse make use of the same apartment, nor doth the King in this respect affect more grandeur than his subjects. When we entered, we seated ourselves on the ground with our legs crossed, in imitation of the rest, whom we found in the same posture. After we had waited some time, the King came in, attended by his domestics and his officers. He held a small lance in his hand, and was dressed in a silk robe, with a turban on his head, to which were fastened some rings of very neat workmanship, which fell down upon his forehead. All kept silence for some time, and the King told us by his interpreter that we were welcome to his dominions, that he had been informed we were to come by the Emperor his father, and that he condoled the hardships we had undergone at sea. He desired us not to be under any concern at finding ourselves in a country so distant from our own, for those dominions were ours, and he and the Emperor his father would give us all the proofs we could desire of the sincerest affection. We returned him thanks for this promise of his favour, and after a short conversation went away. Immediately we were teazed by those who brought us the mules, and demanded to be paid the hire of them; and had advice given us at the same time that we should get a present ready for the King. The Chec Furt, who was extremely ready to undertake any commission of this kind, would needs direct us in the affair, and told us that our gifts ought to be of greater value, because we had neglected making any such offer at our first audience, contrary to the custom of that country. By these pretences he obliged us to make a present to the value of about twenty pounds, with which he seemed to be pleased, and told us we had nothing to do but prepare to make our entry.

CHAPTER VI

The King refuses their present. The author's boldness. The present is afterwards accepted. The people are forbidden to sell them provisions. The author remonstrates against the usage. The King redresses it.

But such was either the hatred or avarice of this man, that instead of doing us the good offices he pretended, he advised the King to refuse our present, that he might draw from us something more valuable. When I attended the King in order to deliver the presents, after I had excused the smallness of them, as being, though unworthy his acceptance, the largest that our profession of poverty, and distance from our country, allowed us to make, he examined them one by one with a dissatisfied look, and told me that however he might be pleased with our good attentions, he thought our present such as could not be offered to a king without affronting him; and made me a sign with his hand to withdraw, and take back what I had brought. I obeyed, telling him that perhaps he might send for it again without having so much. The Chec Furt, who had been the occasion of all this, coming to us afterwards, blamed us exceedingly for having offered so little, and being told by us that the present was picked out by himself, that we had nothing better to give, and that what we had left would scarce defray the expenses of our journey, he pressed us at least to add something, but could prevail no farther than to persuade us to repeat our former offer, which the King was now pleased to accept, though with no kinder countenance than before.

Here we spent our time and our provisions, without being able to procure any more. The country indeed affords goats and honey, but nobody would sell us any, the King, as I was secretly informed, having strictly prohibited it, with a view of forcing all we had from us. The patriarch sent me to expostulate the matter with the King, which I did in very warm terms, telling him that we were assured by the Emperor of a reception in this country far different from what we met with, which assurances he had confirmed by his promise and the civilities we were entertained with at our first arrival; but that instead of friends who would compassionate our miseries, and supply our necessities, we found ourselves in the midst of mortal enemies that wanted to destroy us.

The King, who affected to appear ignorant of the whole affair, demanded an account of the injuries I complained of, and told me that if any of his subjects should dare to attempt our lives, it should cost him his own. We were not, replied I, in danger of being stabbed or poisoned, but are doomed to a more lingering and painful death by that prohibition which obliges your subjects to deny us the necessaries of life; if it be Your Highness's pleasure that we die here, we entreat that we may at least be despatched quickly, and not condemned to longer torments. The King, startled at this discourse, denied that he had given any such orders, and was very importunate to know the author of our intelligence, but finding me determined not to discover him, he sent me away with a promise that for the future we should be furnished with everything we wanted, and indeed that same day we bought three goats for about a crown, and some honey, and found ourselves better treated than before.

CHAPTER VII

They obtain leave, with some difficulty, to depart from Dancali. The difficulties of their march. A broil with the Moors. They arrive at the plain of salt.

This usage, with some differences we had with a Moor, made us very desirous of leaving this country, but we were still put off with one pretence or other whenever we asked leave to depart. Tired with these delays, I applied myself to his favourite minister, with a promise of a large present if he could obtain us an audience of leave; he came to us at night to agree upon the reward, and soon accomplished all we desired, both getting us a permission to go out of the kingdom, and procuring us camels to carry our baggage, and that of the Abyssinian ambassadors who were ordered to accompany us.

We set out from the kingdom of Dancali on the 15th of June, having taken our leave of the King, who after many excuses for everything that had happened, dismissed us with a present of a cow, and some provisions, desiring us to tell the Emperor of Fthiopia his father that we had met with kind treatment in his territories, a request which we did not at that time think it convenient to deny.

Whatever we had suffered hitherto, was nothing to the difficulties we were now entering upon, and which God had decreed us to undergo for the sake of Jesus Christ. Our way now lay through a region scarce passable, and full of serpents, which were continually creeping between our legs; we might have avoided them in the day, but being obliged, that we might avoid the excessive heats, to take long marches in the night, we were every moment treading upon them. Nothing but a signal interposition of Providence could have preserved us from being bitten by them, or perishing either by weariness or thirst, for sometimes we were a long time without water, and had nothing to support our strength in this fatigue but a little honey, and a small piece of cows' flesh dried in the sun. Thus we travelled on for many days, scarce allowing ourselves any rest, till we came to a channel or hollow worn in the mountains by the winter torrents; here we found some coolness, and good water, a blessing we enjoyed for three days; down this channel all the winter runs a great river which is dried up in the heats, or to speak more properly, hides itself under ground. We walked along its side, sometimes seven or eight leagues without seeing any water, and then we found it rising out of the ground, at which places we never failed to drink as much as we could, and fill our bottles.

In our march, there fell out an unlucky accident, which, however, did not prove of the bad consequence it might have done. The master of our camels was an old Mohammedan, who had conceived an opinion that it was an act of merit to do us all the mischief he could; and in pursuance of his notion, made it his chief employment to steal everything he could lay hold on; his piety even transported him so far, that one morning he stole and hid the cords of our tents. The patriarch who saw him at the work charged him with it, and upon his denial, showed him the end of the cord hanging from under the saddle of one of his camels. Upon this we went to seize them, but were opposed by him and the rest of the drivers, who set themselves in a posture of opposition with their daggers. Our soldiers had recourse to their muskets, and four of them putting the mouths of their pieces to the heads of some of the most obstinate

and turbulent, struck them with such a terror, that all the clamour
was stilled in an instant; none received any hurt but the Moor who
had been the occasion of the tumult. He was knocked down by one
of our soldiers, who had cut his throat but that the fathers prevented it: he then restored the cords, and was more tractable ever after.
In all my dealings with the Moors, I have always discovered in
them an ill-natured cowardice, which makes them insupportably
insolent if you show them the least respect, and easily reduced to
reasonable terms when you treat them with a high hand.

After a march of some days we came to an opening between the
mountains, the only passage out of Dancali into Abyssinia. Heaven
seems to have made this place on purpose for the repose of weary
travellers, who here exchange the tortures of parching thirst, burning sands, and a sultry climate, for the pleasures of shady trees, the
refreshment of a clear stream, and the luxury of a cooling breeze.
We arrived at this happy place about noon, and the next day at
evening left those fanning winds, and woods flourishing with un-
fading verdure, for the dismal barrenness of the vast uninhabitable
plains, from which Abyssinia is supplied with salt. These plains are
surrounded with high mountains, continually covered with thick
clouds which the sun draws from the lakes that are here, from
which the water runs down into the plain, and is there congealed
into salt. Nothing can be more curious than to see the channels and
aqueducts that nature has formed in this hard rock, so exact and of
such admirable contrivance, that they seem to be the work of men.
To this place caravans of Abyssinia are continually resorting, to
carry salt into all parts of the empire, which they set a great value
upon, and which in their country is of the same use as money. The
superstitious Abyssins imagine that the cavities of the mountains
are inhabited by evil spirits which appear in different shapes, calling those that pass by their names as in a familiar acquaintance,
who, if they go to them, are never seen afterwards. This relation was
confirmed by the Moorish officer who came with us, who, as he
said, had lost a servant in that manner: the man certainly fell into
the hands of the Galles, who lurk in those dark retreats, cut the
throats of the merchants, and carry off their effects.

The heat making it impossible to travel through this plain in the
day-time, we set out in the evening, and in the night lost our way. It

is very dangerous to go through this place, for there are no marks of the right road, but some heaps of salt, which we could not see. Our camel drivers getting together to consult on this occasion, we suspected they had some ill design in hand, and got ready our weapons; they perceived our apprehensions, and set us at ease by letting us know the reason of their consultation. Travelling hard all night, we found ourselves next morning past the plain; but the road we were in was not more commodious, the points of the rocks pierced our feet; to increase our perplexities we were alarmed with the approach of an armed troop, which our fear immediately suggested to be the Galles, who chiefly beset these passes of the mountains; we put ourselves on the defensive, and expected them, whom, upon a more exact examination, we found to be only a caravan of merchants come as usual to fetch salt.

CHAPTER VIII

They lose their way, are in continual apprehensions of the Galles. They come to Duan, and settle in Abyssinia.

About nine the next morning we came to the end of this toilsome and rugged path, where the way divided into two, yet both led to a well, the only one that was found in our journey. A Moor with three others took the shortest, without directing us to follow him; so we marched forwards we knew not whither, through woods and over rocks, without sleep or any other refreshment: at noon the next day we discovered that we were near the field of salt. Our affliction and distress is not to be expressed; we were all fainting with heat and weariness, and two of the patriarch's servants were upon the point of dying for want of water. None of us had any but a Moor, who could not be prevailed upon to part with it at less than the weight in gold; we got some from him at last, and endeavoured to revive the two servants, while part of us went to look for a guide that might put us in the right way. The Moors who had arrived at the well, rightly guessing that we were lost, sent one of their company to look for us, whom we heard shouting in the woods, but durst make no answer for fear of the Galles. At length he found us, and conducted us to the rest; we instantly forgot our past calamities, and had no other care than to recover the patriarch's attendants. We did not give them a full draught at first, but poured in the water by drops, to moisten their mouths and throats, which were extremely swelled: by this caution they were soon well. We then fell to eating and drinking, and though we had nothing but our ordinary repast of honey and dried flesh, thought we never had regaled more pleasantly in our lives.

We durst not stay long in this place for fear of the Galles, who lay their ambushes more particularly near this well, by which all caravans must necessarily pass. Our apprehensions were very much increased by our suspicion of the camel-drivers, who, as we imagined, had advertised the Galles of our arrival. The fatigue we had already suffered did not prevent our continuing our march all night: at last we entered a plain, where our drivers told us we might expect to be attacked by the Galles; nor was it long before our own eyes convinced us that we were in great danger, for we saw as we went along the dead bodies of a caravan who had been lately massacred, a sight which froze our blood, and filled us with pity and with horror. The same fate was not far from overtaking us, for a troop of Galles, who were detached in search of us, missed us but an hour or two. We spent the next night in the mountains, but when we should have set out in the morning, were obliged to a fierce dispute with the old Moor, who had not yet lost his inclination to destroy us; he would have had us taken a road which was full of those people we were so much afraid of: at length finding he could not prevail with us, that we charged the goods upon him as belonging to the Emperor, to whom he should be answerable for the loss of them, he consented, in a sullen way, to go with us.

The desire of getting out of the reach of the Galles made us press forward with great expedition, and, indeed, fear having entirely engrossed our minds, we were perhaps less sensible of all our labours and difficulties; so violent an apprehension of one danger made us look on many others with unconcern; our pains at last found some intermission at the foot of the mountains of Duan, the frontier of Abyssinia, which separates it from the country of the Moors, through which we had travelled.

Here we imagined we might repose securely, a felicity we had long been strangers to. Here we began to rejoice at the conclusion of our labours; the place was cool and pleasant, the water was excellent, and the birds melodious. Some of our company went into the wood to divert themselves with hearing the birds and frightening the monkeys, creatures so cunning that they would not stir if a man came unarmed, but would run immediately when they saw a gun. At this place our camel drivers left us, to go to the feast of St. Michael, which the Fthiopians celebrate the 16th of June. We persuaded them, however, to leave us their camels and four of their company to take care of them.

We had not waited many days before some messengers came to us with an account that Father Baradas, with the Emperor's nephew, and many other persons of distinction, waited for us at some distance; we loaded our camels, and following the course of the river, came in seven hours to the place we were directed to halt at. Father Manuel Baradas and all the company, who had waited for us a considerable time on the top of the mountain, came down when they saw our tents, and congratulated our arrival. It is not easy to express the benevolence and tenderness with which they embraced us, and the concern they showed at seeing us worn away with hunger, labour, and weariness, our clothes tattered, and our feet bloody.

We left this place of interview the next day, and on the 21st of June arrived at Fremone, the residence of the missionaries, where we were welcomed by great numbers of Catholics, both Portuguese and Abyssins, who spared no endeavours to make us forget all we had suffered in so hazardous a journey, undertaken with no other intention than to conduct them in the way of salvation.

PART II — A DESCRIPTION OF ABYSSINIA

CHAPTER I

The history of Abyssinia. An account of the Queen of Sheba, and of Queen Candace. The conversion of the Abyssins.

The original of the Abyssins, like that of all other nations, is obscure and uncertain. The tradition generally received derives them from Cham, the son of Noah, and they pretend, however improbably, that from his time till now the legal succession of their kings hath never been interrupted, and that the supreme power hath always continued in the same family. An authentic genealogy traced up so high could not but be extremely curious; and with good reason might the Emperors of Abyssinia boast themselves the most illustrious and ancient family in the world. But there are no real grounds for imagining that Providence has vouchsafed them so distinguishing a protection, and from the wars with which this empire hath been shaken in these latter ages we may justly believe that, like all others, it has suffered its revolutions, and that the history of the Abyssins is corrupted with fables. This empire is known by the name of the kingdom of Prester-John. For the Portuguese having heard such wonderful relations of an ancient and famous Christian state called by that name, in the Indies, imagined it could be none but this of Fthiopia. Many things concurred to make them of this opinion: there was no Christian kingdom or state in the Indies of which all was true which they heard of this land of Prester-John: and there was none in the other parts of the world who was a Christian separated from the Catholic Church but what was known, except this kingdom of Fthiopia. It has therefore passed for the kingdom of Prester-John since the time that it was discovered by the Portuguese in the reign of King John the Second.

The country is properly called Abyssinia, and the people term themselves Abyssins. Their histories count a hundred and sixty-two reigns, from Cham to Faciladas or Basilides; among which some women are remarkably celebrated. One of the most renowned is the Queen of Sheba, mentioned in Scripture, whom the natives call Nicaula or Macheda, and in their translation of the gospel, Nagista Azeb, which in their language is Queen of the South. They still show the ruins of a city which appears to have been once of note, as the place where she kept her court, and a village which, from its being the place of her birth, they call the land of Saba. The Kings of Fthiopia draw their boasted pedigree from Minilech, the son of this Queen and Solomon. The other Queen for whom they retain a great veneration is Candace, whom they call Judith, and indeed if what they relate of her could be proved, there never was, amongst the most illustrious and beneficent sovereigns, any to whom their country was more indebted, for it is said that she being converted by Inda her eunuch, whom St. Philip baptised, prevailed with her subjects to quit the worship of idols, and profess the faith of Jesus Christ. This opinion appears to me without any better foundation than another of the conversion of the Abyssins to the Jewish rites by the Queen of Sheba, at her return from the court of Solomon. They, however, who patronise these traditions give us very specious accounts of the zeal and piety of the Abyssins at their first conversion. Many, they say, abandoned all the pleasures and vanities of life for solitude and religious austerities; others devoted themselves to God in an ecclesiastical life; they who could not do these set apart their revenues for building churches, endowing chapels, and founding monasteries, and spent their wealth in costly ornaments for the churches and vessels for the altars. It is true that this people has a natural disposition to goodness; they are very liberal of their alms, they much frequent their churches, and are very studious to adorn them; they practise fasting and other mortifications, and notwithstanding their separation from the Roman Church, and the corruptions which have crept into their faith, yet retain in a great measure the devout fervour of the primitive Christians. There never were greater hopes of uniting this people to the Church of Rome, which their adherence to the Eutichian heresy has made very difficult, than in the time of Sultan Segued, who called us into his dominions in the year 1625, from whence we were expelled in 1634. As I have lived a long time in this country, and borne a share in all that has passed, I will present the reader with a short account of what I have observed, and of the revolution which forced us to abandon Fthiopia, and destroyed all our hopes of reuniting this kingdom with the Roman Church.

The empire of Abyssinia hath been one of the largest which history gives us an account of: it extended formerly from the Red Sea to the kingdom of Congo, and from Egypt to the Indian Sea. It is not long since it contained forty provinces; but is now not much bigger than all Spain, and consists but of five kingdoms and six provinces, of which part is entirely subject to the Emperor, and part only pays him some tribute, or acknowledgment of dependence, either voluntarily or by compulsion. Some of these are of very large extent: the kingdoms of Tigre, Bagameder, and Goiama are as big as Portugal, or bigger; Amhara and Damote are something less. The provinces are inhabited by Moors, Pagans, Jews, and Christians: the last is the reigning and established religion. This diversity of people and religion is the reason that the kingdom in different parts is under different forms of government, and that their laws and customs are extremely various.

The inhabitants of the kingdom of Amhara are the most civilised and polite; and next to them the natives of Tigre, or the true Abyssins. The rest, except the Damotes, the Gasates, and the Agaus, which approach somewhat nearer to civility, are entirely rude and barbarous. Among these nations the Galles, who first alarmed the world in 1542, have remarkably distinguished themselves by the ravages they have committed, and the terror they have raised in this part of Africa. They neither sow their lands nor improve them by any kind of culture; but, living upon milk and flesh, encamp like the Arabs without any settled habitation. They practise no rites of worship, though they believe that in the regions above there dwells a Being that governs the world: whether by this Being they mean the sun or the sky is not known; or, indeed, whether they have not some conception of the God that created them. This deity they call in their language Oul. In other matters they are yet more ignorant, and have some customs so contrary even to the laws of nature, as might almost afford reason to doubt whether they are endued with reason. The Christianity professed by the Abyssins is so corrupted with superstitions, errors, and heresies, and so mingled with ceremonies borrowed from the Jews, that little besides the name of Christianity is to be found here; and the thorns may be said to have choked the grain. This proceeds in a great measure from the diversity of religions which are tolerated there, either by negligence or from motives of policy; and the same cause hath produced such various revolutions, revolts, and civil wars within these later ages. For those different sects do not easily admit of an union with each other, or a quiet subjection to the same monarch. The Abyssins cannot properly be said to have either cities or houses; they live either in tents, or in cottages made of straw and clay; for they very rarely build with stone. Their villages or towns consist of these huts; yet even of such villages they have but few, because the grandees, the viceroys, and the Emperor himself are always in the camp, that they may be prepared, upon the most sudden summons, to go where the exigence of affairs demands their presence. And this precaution is no more than necessary for a prince every year engaged either in foreign wars or intestine commotions. These towns have each a governor, whom they call gadare, over whom is the educ, or lieutenant, and both accountable to an officer called the afamacon, or mouth of the King; because he receives the revenues, which he pays into the hands of the relatinafala, or grand master of the household: sometimes the Emperor creates a ratz, or viceroy, general over all the empire, who is superior to all his other officers.

Fthiopia produces very near the same kinds of provisions as Portugal; though, by the extreme laziness of the inhabitants, in a much less quantity: however, there are some roots, herbs, and fruits which grow there much better than in other places. What the ancients imagined of the torrid zone being uninhabitable is so far from being true, that this climate is very temperate: the heats, indeed, are excessive in Congo and Monomotapa, but in Abyssinia they enjoy a perpetual spring, more delicious and charming than that in our country. The blacks here are not ugly like those of the kingdoms I have spoken of, but have better features, and are not without wit and delicacy; their apprehension is quick, and their judgment sound. The heat of the sun, however it may contribute to their colour, is not the only reason of it; there is some peculiarity in the temper and constitution of their bodies, since the same men, transported into cooler climates, produce children very near as black as themselves.

They have here two harvests in the year, which is a sufficient recompense for the small produce of each; one harvest they have in the winter, which lasts through the months of July, August, and September, the other in the spring; their trees are always green, and it is the fault of the inhabitants that they produce so little fruit, the soil being well adapted to all sorts, especially those that come from the Indies. They have in the greatest plenty raisins, peaches, sour pomegranates, and sugarcanes, and some figs. Most of these are ripe about Lent, which the Abyssins keep with great strictness.

After the vegetable products of this country, it seems not improper to mention the animals which are found in it, of which here are as great numbers, of as many different species, as in any country in the world: it is infested with lions of many kinds, among which are many of that which is called the lion royal. I cannot help giving the reader on this occasion a relation of a fact which I was an eyewitness of. A lion having taken his haunt near the place where I lived, killed all the oxen and cows, and did a great deal of other mischief, of which I heard new complaints every day. A servant of mine having taken a resolution to free the country from this destroyer, went out one day with two lances, and after he had been some time in quest of him, found him with his mouth all smeared with the blood of a cow he had just devoured; the man rushed upon him, and thrust his lance into his throat with such violence that it came out between his shoulders; the beast, with one dreadful roar, fell down into a pit, and lay struggling, till my servant despatched him. I measured the body of this lion, and found him twelve feet between the head and the tail.

CHAPTER II

The animals of Abyssinia; the elephant, unicorn, their horses and cows; with a particular account of the moroc.

There are so great numbers of elephants in Abyssinia that in one evening we met three hundred of them in three troops: as they filled up the whole way, we were in great perplexity a long time what measures to take; at length, having implored the protection of that Providence that superintends the whole creation, we went forwards through the midst of them without any injury. Once we met four young elephants, and an old one that played with them, lifting them up with her trunk; they grew enraged on a sudden, and ran upon us: we had no way of securing ourselves but by flight, which, however, would have been fruitless, had not our pursuers been stopped by a deep ditch. The elephants of Fthiopia are of so stupendous a size, that when I was mounted on a large mule I could not reach with my hand within two spans of the top of their backs. In Abyssinia is likewise found the rhinoceros, a mortal enemy to the elephant. In the province of Agaus has been seen the unicorn, that beast so much talked of, and so little known: the prodigious swiftness with which this creature runs from one wood into another has given me no opportunity of examining it particularly, yet I have had so near a sight of it as to be able to give some description of it. The shape is the same with that of a beautiful horse, exact and nicely proportioned, of a bay colour, with a black tail, which in some provinces is long, in others very short: some have long manes hanging to the ground. They are so timorous that they never feed but surrounded with other beasts that defend them. Deer and other defenceless animals often herd about the elephant, which, contenting himself with roots and leaves, preserves those beasts that place themselves, as it were, under his protection, from the rage and fierceness of others that would devour them.

The horses of Abyssinia are excellent; their mules, oxen, and cows are without number, and in these principally consists the wealth of this country. They have a very particular custom, which obliges every man that hath a thousand cows to save every year one day's milk of all his herd, and make a bath with it for his relations, entertaining them afterwards with a splendid feast. This they do so many days each year, as they have thousands of cattle, so that to express how rich any man is, they tell you he bathes so many times. The tribute paid out of their herds to the King, which is not the most inconsiderable of his revenues, is one cow in ten every three years. The beeves are of several kinds; one sort they have without horns, which are of no other use than to carry burthens, and serve instead of mules. Another twice as big as ours which they breed to kill, fattening them with the milk of three or four cows. Their horns are so large, the inhabitants use them for pitchers, and each will hold about five gallons. One of these oxen, fat and ready to be killed, may be bought at most for two crowns. I have purchased five sheep, or five goats with nine kids, for a piece of calico worth about a crown.

The Abyssins have many sort of fowls both wild and tame; some of the former we are yet unacquainted with: there is one of wonderful beauty, which I have seen in no other place except Peru: it has instead of a comb, a short horn upon its head, which is thick and round, and open at the top. The feitan favez, or devil's horse, looks at a distance like a man dressed in feathers; it walks with abundance of majesty, till it finds itself pursued, and then takes wing, and flies away. But amongst all their birds there is none more remarkable than the moroc, or honey-bird, which is furnished by nature with a peculiar instinct or faculty of discovering honey. They have here multitudes of bees of various kinds; some are tame, like ours, and form their combs in hives. Of the wild ones, some place their honey in hollow trees, others hide it in holes in the ground, which they cover so carefully, that though they are commonly in the highway, they are seldom found, unless by the moroc's help, which, when he has discovered any honey, repairs immediately to the road side, and when he sees a traveller, sings, and claps his wings, making many motions to invite him to follow him, and when he perceives him coming, flies before him from tree to tree, till he comes to the place where the bees have stored their treasure, and then begins to sing melodiously. The Abyssin takes the honey, without failing to leave part of it for the bird, to reward him for his information. This kind of honey I have often tasted, and do not find that it differs from the other sorts in anything but colour; it is somewhat blacker. The great quantity of honey that is gathered, and a prodigious number of cows that is kept here, have often made me call Abyssinia a land of honey and butter.

CHAPTER III

The manner of eating in Abyssinia, their dress, their hospitality, and traffic.

The great lords, and even the Emperor himself, maintain their tables with no great expense. The vessels they make use of are black earthenware, which, the older it is, they set a greater value on. Their way of dressing their meat, an European, till he hath been long accustomed to it, can hardly be persuaded to like; everything they eat smells strong and swims with butter. They make no use of either linen or plates. The persons of rank never touch what they eat, but have their meat cut by their pages, and put into their mouths. When they feast a friend they kill an ox, and set immediately a quarter of him raw upon the table (for their most elegant treat is raw beef newly killed) with pepper and salt; the gall of the ox serves them for oil and vinegar; some, to heighten the delicacy of the entertainment, add a kind of sauce, which they call manta, made of what they take out of the guts of the ox; this they set on the fire, with butter, salt, pepper, and onion. Raw beef, thus relished, is their nicest dish, and is eaten by them with the same appetite and pleasure as we eat the best partridges. They have often done me the favour of helping me to some of this sauce, and I had no way to decline eating it besides telling them it was too good for a missionary.

The common drink of the Abyssins is beer and mead, which they drink to excess when they visit one another; nor can there be a greater offence against good manners than to let the guests go away sober: their liquor is always presented by a servant, who drinks first himself, and then gives the cup to the company, in the order of their quality.

The meaner sort of people here dress themselves very plain; they only wear drawers, and a thick garment of cotton, that covers the rest of their bodies: the people of quality, especially those that frequent the court, run into the contrary extreme, and ruin themselves with costly habits. They wear all sorts of silks, and particularly the fine velvets of Turkey.

They love bright and glaring colours, and dress themselves much in the Turkish manner, except that their clothes are wider, and their drawers cover their legs. Their robes are always full of gold and silver embroidery. They are most exact about their hair, which is long and twisted, and their care of it is such that they go bareheaded whilst they are young for fear of spoiling it, but afterwards wear red caps, and sometimes turbans after the Turkish fashion.

The ladies' dress is yet more magnificent and expensive; their robes are as large as those of the religious, of the order of St. Bernard. They have various ways of dressing their heads, and spare no expense in ear-rings, necklaces, or anything that may contribute to set them off to advantage. They are not much reserved or confined, and have so much liberty in visiting one another that their husbands often suffer by it; but for this evil there is no remedy, especially when a man marries a princess, or one of the royal family. Besides their clothes, the Abyssins have no movables or furniture of much value, or doth their manner of living admit of them.

One custom of this country deserves to be remarked: when a stranger comes to a village, or to the camp, the people are obliged to entertain him and his company according to his rank. As soon as he enters a house (for they have no inns in this nation), the master informs his neighbours that he hath a guest; immediately they bring in bread and all kinds of provisions; and there is great care taken to provide enough, because, if the guest complains, the town is obliged to pay double the value of what they ought to have furnished. This practice is so well established that a stranger goes into a house of one he never saw with the same familiarity and assurance of welcome as into that of an intimate friend or near relation; a custom very convenient, but which gives encouragement to great numbers of vagabonds throughout the kingdom.

There is no money in Abyssinia, except in the eastern provinces, where they have iron coin: but in the chief provinces all commerce is managed by exchange. Their chief trade consists in provisions, cows, sheep, goats, fowls, pepper, and gold, which is weighed out to the purchaser, and principally in salt, which is properly the money of this country.

When the Abyssins are engaged in a law-suit, the two parties make choice of a judge, and plead their own cause before him; and if they cannot agree in their choice, the governor of the place appoints them one, from whom there lies an appeal to the viceroy and to the Emperor himself. All causes are determined on the spot; no writings are produced. The judge sits down on the ground in the midst of the high road, where all that please may be present: the two persons concerned stand before him, with their friends about them, who serve as their attorneys. The plaintiff speaks first, the defendant answers him; each is permitted to rejoin three or four times, then silence is commanded, and the judge takes the opinions of those that are about him. If the evidence be deemed sufficient, he pronounces sentence, which in some cases is decisive and without appeal. He then takes the criminal into custody till he hath made satisfaction; but if it be a crime punishable with death he is delivered over to the prosecutor, who may put him to death at his own discretion.

They have here a particular way of punishing adultery; a woman convicted of that crime is condemned to forfeit all her fortune, is turned out of her husband's house, in a mean dress, and is forbid ever to enter it again; she has only a needle given her to get her living with. Sometimes her head is shaved, except one lock of hair, which is left her, and even that depends on the will of her husband, who has it likewise in his choice whether he will receive her again or not; if he resolves never to admit her they are both at liberty to marry whom they will. There is another custom amongst them yet more extraordinary, which is, that the wife is punished whenever the husband proves false to the marriage contract; this punishment indeed extends no farther than a pecuniary mulct, and what seems more equitable, the husband is obliged to pay a sum of money to his wife. When the husband prosecutes his wife's gallant, if he can produce any proofs of a criminal conversation, he recovers for damages forty cows, forty horses, and forty suits of clothes, and the same number of other things. If the gallant be unable to pay him, he is committed to prison, and continues there during the husband's pleasure, who, if he sets him at liberty before the whole fine be paid, obliges him to take an oath that he is going to procure the rest, that he may be able to make full satisfaction. Then the criminal orders meat and drink to be brought out, they eat and drink together, he asks a formal pardon, which is not granted at first; however, the husband forgives first one part of the debt, and then another, till at length the whole is remitted.

A husband that doth not like his wife may easily find means to make the marriage void, and, what is worse, may dismiss the second wife with less difficulty than he took her, and return to the first; so that marriages in this country are only for a term of years, and last no longer than both parties are pleased with each other, which is one instance how far distant these people are from the purity of the primitive believers, which they pretend to have preserved with so great strictness. The marriages are in short no more than bargains, made with this proviso, that when any discontent shall arise on either side, they may separate, and marry whom they please, each taking back what they brought with them.

CHAPTER IV

An account of the religion of the Abyssins.

Yet though there is a great difference between our manners, customs, civil government, and those of the Abyssins, there is yet a much greater in points of faith; for so many errors have been introduced and ingrafted into their religion, by their ignorance, their separation from the Catholic Church, and their intercourse with Jews, Pagans, and Mohammedans, that their present religion is nothing but a kind of confused miscellany of Jewish and Mohammedan superstitions, with which they have corrupted those remnants of Christianity which they still retain.

They have, however, preserved the belief of our principal mysteries; they celebrate with a great deal of piety the passion of our Lord; they reverence the cross; they pay a great devotion to the Blessed Virgin, the angels, and the saints; they observe the festivals, and pay a strict regard to the Sunday. Every month they commemorate the assumption of the Virgin Mary, and are of opinion that no Christians beside themselves have a true sense of the greatness of the mother of God, or pay her the honours that are due to her. There are some tribes amongst them (for they are distinguished like the Jews by their tribes), among whom the crime of swearing by the name of the Virgin is punished with forfeiture of goods and even with loss of life; they are equally scrupulous of swearing by St. George. Every week they keep a feast to the honour of the apostles and angels; they come to mass with great devotion, and love to hear the word of God. They receive the sacrament often, but do not always prepare themselves by confession. Their charity to the poor may be said to exceed the proper bounds that prudence ought to set it, for it contributes to encourage great numbers of beggars, which are a great annoyance to the whole kingdom, and as I have often said, afford more exercise to a Christian's patience than his charity; for their insolence is such, that they will refuse what is offered them if it be not so much as they think proper to ask.

Though the Abyssins have not many images, they have great numbers of pictures, and perhaps pay them somewhat too high a degree of worship. The severity of their fasts is equal to that of the primitive church. In Lent they never eat till after sunset; their fasts are the more severe because milk and butter are forbidden them, and no reason or necessity whatsoever can procure them a permission to eat meat, and their country affording no fish, they live only on roots and pulse. On fast-days they never drink but at their meat, and the priests never communicate till evening, for fear of profaning them. They do not think themselves obliged to fast till they have children either married or fit to be married, which yet doth not secure them very long from these mortifications, because their youths marry at the age of ten years, and their girls younger.

There is no nation where excommunication carries greater terrors than among the Abyssins, which puts it in the power of the priests to abuse this religious temper of the people, as well as the authority they receive from it, by excommunicating them, as they often do, for the least trifle in which their interest is concerned.

No country in the world is so full of churches, monasteries, and ecclesiastics as Abyssinia; it is not possible to sing in one church or monastery without being heard by another, and perhaps by several. They sing the psalms of David, of which, as well as the other parts of the Holy Scriptures, they have a very exact translation in their own language; in which, though accounted canonical, the books of the Maccabees are omitted. The instruments of music made use of in their rites of worship are little drums, which they hang about their necks, and beat with both their hands; these are carried even by their chief men, and by the gravest of their ecclesiastics. They have sticks likewise, with which they strike the ground, accompanying the blow with a motion of their whole bodies. They begin their concert by stamping their feet on the ground, and playing gently on their instruments; but when they have heated themselves by degrees, they leave off drumming, and fall to leaping, dancing, and clapping their hands, at the same time straining their voices to the utmost pitch, till at length they have no regard either to the tune or the pauses, and seem rather a riotous than a religious assembly. For this manner of worship they cite the psalm of David, "O clap your hands all ye nations." Thus they misapply the sacred writings to defend practices yet more corrupt than those I have been speaking of.

They are possessed with a strange notion that they are the only true Christians in the world; as for us, they shunned us as heretics, and were under the greatest surprise at hearing us mention the Virgin Mary with the respect which is due to her, and told us that we could not be entirely barbarians since we were acquainted with the mother of God. It plainly appears that prepossessions so strong, which receive more strength from the ignorance of the people, have very little tendency to dispose them to a reunion with the Catholic Church.

They have some opinions peculiar to themselves about purgatory, the creation of souls, and some of our mysteries. They repeat baptism every year, they retain the practice of circumcision, they observe the Sabbath, they abstain from all those sorts of flesh which are forbidden by the law. Brothers espouse the wives of their brothers, and to conclude, they observe a great number of Jewish ceremonies.

Though they know the words which Jesus Christ appointed to be used in the administration of baptism, they have without scruple substituted others in their place, which makes the validity of their baptism, and the reality of their Christianity, very doubtful. They have a few names of saints, the same with those in the Roman martyrology, but they often insert others, as Zama la Cota, the Life of Truth; Ongulari, the Evangelist; Asca Georgi, the Mouth of Saint George.

To bring back this people into the enclosure of the Catholic Church, from which they have been separated so many ages, was the sole view and intention with which we undertook so long and toilsome a journey, crossed so many seas, and passed so many deserts, with the utmost hazard of our lives; I am certain that we travelled more than seven thousand leagues before we arrived at our residence at Fremona.

We came to this place, anciently called Maigoga, on the 21st of June, as I have said before, and were obliged to continue there till November, because the winter begins here in May, and its greatest rigour is from the middle of June to the middle of September. The rains that are almost continually falling in this season make it impossible to go far from home, for the rivers overflow their banks, and therefore, in a place like this, where there are neither bridges nor boats, are, if they are not fordable, utterly impassable. Some, indeed, have crossed them by means of a cord fastened on both sides of the water, others tie two beams together, and placing themselves upon them, guide them as well as they can, but this experiment is so dangerous that it hath cost many of these bold adventurers their lives. This is not all the danger, for there is yet more to be apprehended from the unwholesomeness of the air, and the vapours which arise from the scorched earth at the fall of the first showers, than from the torrents and rivers. Even they who shelter themselves in houses find great difficulty to avoid the diseases that proceed from the noxious qualities of these vapours. From the beginning of June to that of September it rains more or less every day. The morning is generally fair and bright, but about two hours after noon the sky is clouded, and immediately succeeds a violent storm, with thunder and lightning flashing in the most dreadful manner. While this lasts, which is commonly three or four hours, none go out of doors. The ploughman upon the first appearance of it unyokes his oxen, and betakes himself with them into covert. Travellers provide for their security in the neighbouring villages, or set up their tents, everybody flies to some shelter, as well to avoid the unwholesomeness as the violence of the rain. The thunder is astonishing, and the lightning often destroys great numbers, a thing I can speak of from my own experience, for it once flashed so near me, that I felt an uneasiness on that side for a long time after; at the same time it killed three young children, and having run round my room went out, and killed a man and woman three hundred paces off. When the storm is over the sun shines out as before, and one would not imagine it had rained, but that the ground appears deluged. Thus passes the Abyssinian winter, a dreadful season, in which the whole kingdom languishes with numberless diseases, an affliction which, however grievous, is yet equalled by the clouds of grasshoppers, which fly in such numbers from the desert, that the sun is hid and the sky darkened; whenever this plague appears, nothing is seen through the whole region but the most ghastly consternation, or heard but the most piercing lamentations, for wherever they fall, that unhappy place is laid waste and ruined; they leave not one blade of grass, nor any hopes of a harvest.

God, who often makes calamities subservient to His will, permitted this very affliction to be the cause of the conversion of many of the natives, who might have otherwise died in their errors; for part of the country being ruined by the grasshoppers that year in which we arrived at Abyssinia, many, who were forced to leave their habitations, and seek the necessaries of life in other places, came to that part of the land where some of our missionaries were preaching, and laid hold on that mercy which God seemed to have appointed for others.

As we could not go to court before November, we resolved, that we might not be idle, to preach and instruct the people in the country; in pursuance of this resolution I was sent to a mountain, two days' journey distant from Maigoga. The lord or governor of the place was a Catholic, and had desired missionaries, but his wife had conceived an implacable aversion both from us and the Roman Church, and almost all the inhabitants of that mountain were infected with the same prejudices as she. They had been persuaded that the hosts which we consecrated and gave to the communicants were mixed with juices strained from the flesh of a camel, a dog, a hare, and a swine; all creatures which the Abyssins look upon with abhorrence, believing them unclean, and forbidden to them, as they were to the Jews. We had no way of undeceiving them, and they fled from us whenever we approached. We carried with us our tent, our chalices, and ornaments, and all that was necessary for saying mass. The lord of the village, who, like other persons of quality throughout Fthiopia, lived on the top of a mountain, received us with very great civility. All that depended upon him had built their huts round about him; so that this place compared with the other towns of Abyssinia seems considerable; as soon as we arrived he sent us his compliments, with a present of a cow, which, among them, is a token of high respect. We had no way of returning this favour but by killing the cow, and sending a quarter smoking, with the gall, which amongst them is esteemed the most delicate part. I imagined for some time that the gall of animals was less bitter in this country than elsewhere, but upon tasting it, I found it more;

and yet have frequently seen our servants drink large glasses of if with the same pleasure that we drink the most delicious wines.

We chose to begin our mission with the lady of the village, and hoped that her prejudice and obstinacy, however great, would in time yield to the advice and example of her husband, and that her conversion would have a great influence on the whole village, but having lost several days without being able to prevail upon her to hear us on any one point, we left the place, and went to another mountain, higher and better peopled. When we came to the village on the top of it, where the lord lived, we were surprised with the cries and lamentations of men that seemed to suffer or apprehend some dreadful calamity; and were told, upon inquiring the cause, that the inhabitants had been persuaded that we were the devil's missionaries, who came to seduce them from the true religion, that foreseeing some of their neighbours would be ruined by the temptation, they were lamenting the misfortune which was coming upon them. When we began to apply ourselves to the work of the mission we could not by any means persuade any but the lord and the priest to receive us into their houses; the rest were rough and untractable to that degree that, after having converted six, we despaired of making any farther progress, and thought it best to remove to other towns where we might be better received.

We found, however, a more unpleasing treatment at the next place, and had certainly ended our lives there had we not been protected by the governor and the priest, who, though not reconciled to the Roman Church, yet showed us the utmost civility; the governor informed us of a design against our lives, and advised us not to go out after sunset, and gave us guards to protect us from the insults of the populace.

We made no long stay in a place where they stopped their ears against the voice of God, but returned to the foot of that mountain which we had left some days before; we were surrounded, as soon as we began to preach, with a multitude of auditors, who came either in expectation of being instructed, or from a desire of gratifying their curiosity, and God bestowed such a blessing upon our apostolical labours that the whole village was converted in a short time. We then removed to another at the middle of the mountain, situated in a kind of natural parterre, or garden; the soil was fruitful, and the trees that shaded it from the scorching heat of the sun gave it an agreeable and refreshing coolness. We had here the convenience of improving the ardour and piety of our new converts, and, at the same time, of leading more into the way of the true religion: and indeed our success exceeded the utmost of our hopes; we had in a short time great numbers whom we thought capable of being admitted to the sacraments of baptism and the mass.

We erected our tent, and placed our altar under some great trees, for the benefit of the shade; and every day before sun-rising my companion and I began to catechise and instruct these new Catholics, and used our utmost endeavours to make them abjure their errors. When we were weary with speaking, we placed in ranks those who were sufficiently instructed, and passing through them with great vessels of water, baptised them according to the form prescribed by the Church. As their number was very great, we cried aloud, those of this rank are named Peter, those of that rank Anthony. And did the same amongst the women, whom we separated from the men. We then confessed them, and admitted them to the communion. After mass we applied ourselves again to catechise, to instruct, and receive the renunciation of their errors, scarce allowing ourselves time to make a scanty meal, which we never did more than once a day.

After some time had been spent here, we removed to another town not far distant, and continued the same practice. Here I was accosted one day by an inhabitant of that place, where he had found the people so prejudiced against us, who desired to be admitted to confession. I could not forbear asking him some questions about those lamentations, which we heard upon our entering into that place. He confessed with the utmost frankness and ingenuity that the priests and religious have given dreadful accounts both of us and of the religion we preached; that the unhappy people were taught by them that the curse of God attended us wheresoever we went; that we were always followed by the grasshoppers, that pest of Abyssinia, which carried famine and destruction over all the country; that he, seeing no grasshoppers following us when we passed by their village, began to doubt of the reality of what the priests had so confidently asserted, and was now convinced that the representation they made of us was calumny and imposture. This discourse gave us double pleasure, both as it proved that God had confuted the accusations of our enemies, and defended us against their malice without any efforts of our own, and that the people who had shunned us with the strongest detestation were yet lovers of truth, and came to us on their own accord. Nothing could be more grossly absurd than the reproaches which the Abyssinian ecclesiastics aspersed us and our religion with. They had taken advantage of the calamity that happened the year of our arrival: and the Abyssins, with all their wit, did not consider that they had often been distressed by the grasshoppers before there came any Jesuits into the country, and indeed before there were any in the world.

Whilst I was in these mountains, I went on Sundays and saints' days sometimes to one church and sometimes to another. One day I went out with a resolution not to go to a certain church, where I imagined there was no occasion for me, but before I had gone far, I found myself pressed by a secret impulse to return back to that same church. I obeyed the influence, and discovered it to proceed from the mercy of God to three young children who were destitute of all succour, and at the point of death. I found two very quickly in this miserable state; the mother had retired to some distance that she might not see them die, and when she saw me stop, came and told me that they had been obliged by want to leave the town they lived in, and were at length reduced to this dismal condition, that she had been baptised, but that the children had not. After I had baptised and relieved them, I continued my walk, reflecting with wonder on the mercy of God, and about evening discovered another infant, whose mother, evidently a Catholic, cried out to me to save her child, or at least that if I could not preserve this uncertain and perishable life, I should give it another certain and permanent. I sent my servant to fetch water with the utmost expedition, for there was none near, and happily baptised the child before it expired.

Soon after this I returned to Fremona, and had great hopes of accompanying the patriarch to the court; but, when we were almost setting out, received the command of the superior of the mission to stay at Fremona, with a charge of the house there, and of all the Catholics that were dispersed over the kingdom of Tigre, an employment very ill-proportioned to my abilities. The house at Fremona has always been much regarded even by those emperors who persecuted us; Sultan Segued annexed nine large manors to it for ever, which did not make us much more wealthy, because of the expensive hospitality which the great conflux of strangers obliged us to. The lands in Abyssinia yield but small revenues, unless the owners themselves set the value upon them, which we could not do.

The manner of letting farms in Abyssinia differs much from that of other countries: the farmer, when the harvest is almost ripe, invites the chumo or steward, who is appointed to make an estimate of the value of each year's product, to his house, entertains him in the most agreeable manner he can; makes him a present, and then takes him to see his corn. If the chumo is pleased with the treat and present, he will give him a declaration or writing to witness that his ground, which afforded five or six sacks of corn, did you yield so many bushels, and even of this it is the custom to abate something; so that our revenue did not increase in proportion to our lands; and we found ourselves often obliged to buy corn, which, indeed, is not dear, for in fruitful years forty or fifty measures, weighing each about twenty-two pounds, may be purchased for a crown.

Besides the particular charge I had of the house of Fremona, I was appointed the patriarch's grand-vicar through the whole kingdom of Tigre. I thought that to discharge this office as I ought, it was incumbent on me to provide necessaries as well for the bodies as the souls of the converted Catholics. This labour was much increased by the famine which the grasshoppers had brought that year upon the country. Our house was perpetually surrounded by some of those unhappy people, whom want had compelled to abandon their habitations, and whose pale cheeks and meagre bodies were undeniable proofs of their misery and distress. All the relief I could possibly afford them could not prevent the death of such numbers that their bodies filled the highways; and to increase our affliction, the wolves having devoured the carcases, and finding no other food, fell upon the living; their natural fierceness being so increased by hunger, that they dragged the children out of the very houses. I saw myself a troop of wolves tear a child of six years old in pieces before I or any one else could come to its assistance.

While I was entirely taken up with the duties of my ministry, the viceroy of Tigre received the commands of the Emperor to search for the bones of Don Christopher de Gama. On this occasion it may not be thought impertinent to give some account of the life and death of this brave and holy Portuguese, who, after having been successful in many battles, fell at last into the hands of the Moors, and completed that illustrious life by a glorious martyrdom.

CHAPTER V

The adventures of the Portuguese, and the actions of Don Christopher de Gama in Fthiopia.

About the beginning of the sixteenth century arose a Moor near the Cape of Gardafui, who, by the assistance of the forces sent him from Moca by the Arabs and Turks, conquered almost all Abyssinia, and founded the kingdom of Adel. He was called Mahomet Gragne, or the Lame. When he had ravaged Fthiopia fourteen years, and was master of the greatest part of it, the Emperor David sent to implore succour of the King of Portugal, with a promise that when those dominions were recovered which had been taken from him, he would entirely submit himself to the Pope, and resign the third part of his territories to the Portuguese. After many delays, occasioned by the great distance between Portugal and Abyssinia, and some unsuccessful attempts, King John the Third, having made Don Stephen de Gama, son of the celebrated Don Vasco de Gama, viceroy of the Indies, gave him orders to enter the Red Sea in pursuit of the Turkish galleys, and to fall upon them wherever he found them, even in the Port of Suez. The viceroy, in obedience to the king's commands, equipped a powerful fleet, went on board himself, and cruised about the coast without being able to discover the Turkish vessels. Enraged to find that with this great preparation he should be able to effect nothing, he landed at Mazna four hundred Portuguese, under the command of Don Christopher de Gama, his brother. He was soon joined by some Abyssins, who had not yet forgot their allegiance to their sovereign; and in his march up the country was met by the Empress Helena, who received him as her deliverer. At first nothing was able to stand before the valour of the Portuguese, the Moors were driven from one mountain to another, and were dislodged even from those places, which it seemed almost impossible to approach, even unmolested by the opposition of an enemy.

These successes seemed to promise a more happy event than that which followed them. It was now winter, a season in which, as the reader hath been already informed, it is almost impossible to travel in Fthiopia. The Portuguese unadvisedly engaged themselves in an enterprise, to march through the whole country, in order to join the Emperor, who was then in the most remote part of his dominions. Mahomet, who was in possession of the mountains, being informed by his spies that the Portuguese were but four hundred, encamped in the plain of Ballut, and sent a message to the general that he knew the Abyssins had imposed on the King of Portugal, which, being acquainted with their treachery, he was not surprised at, and that in compassion of the commander's youth, he would give him and his men, if they would return, free passage, and furnish them with necessaries; that he might consult upon the matter, and depend upon his word, reminding him, however, that it was not safe to refuse his offer.

The general presented the ambassador with a rich robe, and returned this gallant answer: "That he and his fellow-soldiers were come with an intention to drive Mahomet out of these countries, which he had wrongfully usurped; that his present design was, instead of returning back the way he came, as Mahomet advised, to open himself a passage through the country of his enemies; that Mahomet should rather think of determining whether he would fight or yield up his ill-gotten territories, than of prescribing measures to him; that he put his whole confidence in the omnipotence of God and the justice of his cause, and that to show how just a sense he had of Mahomet's kindness, he took the liberty of presenting him with a looking-glass and a pair of pincers."

This answer, and the present, so provoked Mahomet, who was at dinner when he received it, that he rose from table immediately to march against the Portuguese, imagining he should meet with no resistance; and indeed, any man, however brave, would have been of the same opinion; for his forces consisted of fifteen thousand foot, beside a numerous body of cavalry, and the Portuguese commander had but three hundred and fifty men, having lost eight in attacking some passes, and left forty at Mazma, to maintain an open intercourse with the viceroy of the Indies. This little troop of our countrymen were upon the declivity of a hill near a wood; above them stood the Abyssins, who resolved to remain quiet spectators of the battle, and to declare themselves on that side which should be favoured with victory.

Mahomet began the attack with only ten horsemen, against whom as many Portuguese were detached, who fired with so much exactness, that nine of the Moors fell, and the tenth with great difficulty made his escape. This omen of good fortune gave the soldiers great encouragement; the action grew hot, and they came at length to a general battle; but the Moors, dismayed by the advantages our men had obtained at first, were half defeated before the fight. The great fire of our muskets and artillery broke them immediately. Mahomet preserved his own life not without difficulty, but did not lose his capacity with the battle: he had still a great number of troops remaining, which he rallied, and entrenched himself at Membret, a place naturally strong, with an intention to pass the winter there, and wait for succours.

The Portuguese, who were more desirous of glory than wealth, did not encumber themselves with plunder, but with the utmost expedition pursued their enemies, in hopes of cutting them entirely off. This expectation was too sanguine: they found them encamped in a place naturally almost inaccessible, and so well fortified, that it would be no less than extreme rashness to attack them. They therefore entrenched themselves on a hill over against the enemy's camp, and though victorious, were under great disadvantages. They saw new troops arrive every day at the enemy's camp, and their small number grew less continually; their friends at Mazna could not join them; they knew not how to procure provisions, and could put no confidence in the Abyssins; yet recollecting the great things achieved by their countrymen, and depending on the Divine protection, they made no doubt of surmounting all difficulties.

Mahomet on his part was not idle; he solicited the assistance of the Mahometan princes, pressed them with all the motives of religion, and obtained a reinforcement of two thousand musketeers from the Arabs, and a train of artillery from the Turks. Animated with these succours, he marched out of his trenches to enter those of the Portuguese, who received him with the utmost bravery, destroyed prodigious numbers of his men, and made many sallies with great vigour, but losing every day some of their small troops, and most of their officers being killed, it was easy to surround and force them.

Their general had already one arm broken, and his knee shattered with a musket-shot, which made him unable to repair to all those places where his presence was necessary to animate his soldiers. Valour was at length forced to submit to superiority of numbers; the enemy entered the camp and put all to the sword. The general with ten more escaped the slaughter, and by means of their horses retreated to a wood, where they were soon discovered by a detachment sent in search of them, and brought to Mahomet, who was overjoyed to see his most formidable enemy in his power, and ordered him to take care of his uncle and nephew, who were wounded, telling him he should answer for their lives; and, upon their death, taxed him with hastening it. The brave Portuguese made no excuses, but told him he came thither to destroy Mahometans, and not to save them. Mahomet, enraged at this language, ordered a stone to be put on his head, and exposed this great man to the insults and reproaches of the whole army. After this they inflicted various kinds of tortures on him, which he endured with incredible resolution, and without uttering the least complaint, praising the mercy of God who had ordained him to suffer in such a cause.

Mahomet, at last satisfied with cruelty, made an offer of sending him to the viceroy of the Indies, if he would turn Mussulman. The hero took fire at this proposal, and answered with the highest indignation that nothing should make him forsake his heavenly Master to follow an impostor, and continued in the severest terms to vilify their false prophet, till Mahomet struck off his head.

Nor did the resentment of Mahomet end here; he divided his body into quarters, and sent them to different places. The Catholics gathered the remains of this glorious martyr, and interred them. Every Moor that passed by threw a stone upon his grave, and raised in time such a heap, as I found it difficult to remove when I went in search of those precious relics.

What I have here related of the death of Don Christopher de Gama I was told by an old man, who was an eye-witness of it: and there is a tradition in the country that in the place where his head fell, a fountain sprung up of wonderful virtue, which cured many diseases otherwise past remedy.

CHAPTER VI

Mahomet continues the war, and is killed. The stratagem of Peter Leon.

Mahomet, that he might make the best use of his victory, ranged over a great part of Abyssinia in search of the Emperor Claudius, who was then in the kingdom of Dambia. All places submitted to the Mahometan, whose insolence increased every day with his power; and nothing after the defeat of the Portuguese was supposed able to put a stop to the progress of his arms.

The soldiers of Portugal, having lost their chief, resorted to the Emperor, who, though young, promised great things, and told them that since their own general was dead, they would accept of none but himself. He received them with great kindness, and hearing of Don Christopher de Gama's misfortune, could not forbear honouring with some tears the memory of a man who had come so far to his succour, and lost his life in his cause.

The Portuguese, resolved at any rate to revenge the fate of their general, desired the Emperor to assign them the post opposite to Mahomet, which was willingly granted them. That King, flushed with his victories, and imagining to fight was undoubtedly to conquer, sought all occasions of giving the Abyssins battle. The Portuguese, who desired nothing more than to re-establish their reputation by revenging the affront put upon them by the late defeat, advised the Emperor to lay hold on the first opportunity of fighting. Both parties joined battle with equal fury. The Portuguese directed all their force against that part where Mahomet was posted. Peter Leon, who had been servant to the general, singled the King out among the crowd, and shot him into the head with his musket. Mahomet, finding himself wounded, would have retired out of the battle, and was followed by Peter Leon, till he fell down dead; the Portuguese, alighting from his horse, cut off one of his ears. The

Moors being now without a leader, continued the fight but a little time, and at length fled different ways in the utmost disorder; the Abyssinians pursued them, and made a prodigious slaughter. One of them, seeing the King's body on the ground, cut off his head and presented it to the Emperor. The sight of it filled the whole camp with acclamations; every one applauded the valour and good fortune of the Abyssin, and no reward was thought great enough for so important a service. Peter Leon, having stood by some time, asked whether the King had but one ear? if he had two, says he, it seems likely that the man who killed him cut off one and keeps it as a proof of his exploit. The Abyssin stood confused, and the Portuguese produced the ear out of his pocket. Every one commended the stratagem; and the Emperor commanded the Abyssin to restore all the presents he had received, and delivered them with many more to Peter Leon.

I imagined the reader would not be displeased to be informed who this man was, whose precious remains were searched for by a viceroy of Tigre, at the command of the Emperor himself. The commission was directed to me, nor did I ever receive one that was more welcome on many accounts. I had contracted an intimate friendship with the Count de Vidigueira, viceroy of the Indies, and had been desired by him, when I took my leave of him, upon going to Melinda, to inform myself where his relation was buried, and to send him some of his relics.

The viceroy, son-in-law to the Emperor, with whom I was joined in the commission, gave me many distinguishing proofs of his affection to me, and of his zeal for the Catholic religion. It was a journey of fifteen days through part of the country possessed by the Galles, which made it necessary to take troops with us for our security; yet, notwithstanding this precaution, the hazard of the expedition appeared so great, that our friends bid us farewell with tears, and looked upon us as destined to unavoidable destruction. The viceroy had given orders to some troops to join us on the road, so that our little army grew stronger as we advanced. There is no making long marches in this country; an army here is a great city well peopled and under exact government: they take their wives and children with them, and the camp hath its streets, its market places, its churches, courts of justice, judges, and civil officers.

Before they set forward, they advertise the governors of provinces through which they are to pass, that they may take care to furnish what is necessary for the subsistence of the troops. These governors give notice to the adjacent places that the army is to march that way on such a day, and that they are assessed such a quantity of bread, beer, and cows. The peasants are very exact in supplying their quota, being obliged to pay double the value in case of failure; and very often when they have produced their full share, they are told that they have been deficient, and condemned to buy their peace with a large fine.

When the providore has received these contributions, he divides them according to the number of persons, and the want they are in: the proportion they observe in this distribution is twenty pots of beer, ten of mead, and one cow to a hundred loaves. The chief officers and persons of note carry their own provisions with them, which I did too, though I afterwards found the precaution unnecessary, for I had often two or three cows more than I wanted, which I bestowed on those whose allowance fell short.

The Abyssins are not only obliged to maintain the troops in their march, but to repair the roads, to clear them, especially in the forests, of brambles and thorns, and by all means possible to facilitate the passage of the army. They are, by long custom, extremely ready at encamping. As soon as they come to a place they think convenient to halt at, the officer that commands the vanguard marks out with his pike the place for the King's or viceroy's tent: every one knows his rank, and how much ground he shall take up; so the camp is formed in an instant.

CHAPTER VII

They discover the relics. Their apprehension of the Galles. The author converts a criminal, and procures his pardon.

We took with us an old Moor, so enfeebled with age that they were forced to carry him: he had seen, as I have said, the sufferings and death of Don Christopher de Gama; and a Christian, who had often heard all those passages related to his father, and knew the place where the uncle and nephew of Mahomet were buried, and where they interred one quarter of the Portuguese martyr. We often examined these two men, and always apart; they agreed in every circumstance of their relations, and confirmed us in our belief of them by leading us to the place where we took up the uncle and nephew of Mahomet, as they had described. With no small labour we removed the heap of stones which the Moors, according to their custom, had thrown upon the body, and discovered the treasure we came in search of. Not many paces off was the fountain where they had thrown his head, with a dead dog, to raise a greater aversion in the Moors. I gathered the teeth and the lower jaw. No words can express the ecstasies I was transported with at seeing the relics of so great a man, and reflecting that it had pleased God to make me the instrument of their preservation, so that one day, if our holy father the Pope shall be so pleased, they may receive the veneration of the faithful. All burst into tears at the sight. We indulged a melancholy pleasure in reflecting what that great man had achieved for the deliverance of Abyssinia, from the yoke and tyranny of the Moors; the voyages he had undertaken; the battles he had fought; the victories he had won; and the cruel and tragical death he had suffered. Our first moments were so entirely taken up with these reflections that we were incapable of considering the danger we were in of being immediately surrounded by the Galles; but as soon as we awoke to that thought, we contrived to retreat as fast as we could. Our expedition, however, was not so great but we saw them on the top of a mountain ready to pour down upon us. The viceroy attended us closely with his little army, but had been probably not much more secure than we, his force consisting only of foot, and the Galles entirely of horse, a service at which they are very expert. Our apprehensions at last proved to be needless, for the troops we saw were of a nation at that time in alliance with the Abyssins.

Not caring, after this alarm, to stay longer here, we set out on our march back, and in our return passed through a village where two men, who had murdered a domestic of the viceroy, lay under an arrest. As they had been taken in the fact, the law of the country allowed that they might have been executed the same hour, but the viceroy having ordered that their death should be deferred till his return, delivered them to the relations of the dead, to be disposed of as they should think proper. They made great rejoicings all the night, on account of having it in their power to revenge their relation; and the unhappy criminals had the mortification of standing by to behold this jollity, and the preparations made for their execution.

The Abyssins have three different ways of putting a criminal to death: one way is to bury him to the neck, to lay a heap of brambles upon his head, and to cover the whole with a great stone; another is to beat him to death with cudgels; a third, and the most usual, is to stab him with their lances. The nearest relation gives the first thrust, and is followed by all the rest according to their degrees of kindred; and they to whom it does not happen to strike while the offender is alive, dip the points of their lances in his blood to show that they partake in the revenge. It frequently happens that the relations of the criminal are for taking the like vengeance for his death, and sometimes pursue this resolution so far that all those who had any share in the prosecution lose their lives.

I being informed that these two men were to die, wrote to the viceroy for his permission to exhort them, before they entered into eternity, to unite themselves to the Church. My request being granted, I applied myself to the men, and found one of them so obstinate that he would not even afford me a hearing, and died in his error. The other I found more flexible, and wrought upon him so far that he came to my tent to be instructed. After my care of his eternal welfare had met with such success, I could not forbear attempting something for his temporal, and by my endeavours matters were so accommodated that the relations were willing to grant his life on condition he paid a certain number of cows, or the value. Their first demand was of a thousand; he offered them five; they at last were satisfied with twelve, provided they were paid upon the spot. The Abyssins are extremely charitable, and the women, on such occasions, will give even their necklaces and pendants, so that, with what I gave myself, I collected in the camp enough to pay the fine, and all parties were content.

CHAPTER VIII

The viceroy is offended by his wife. He complains to the Emperor, but without redress. He meditates a revolt, raises an army, and makes an attempt to seize upon the author.

We continued our march, and the viceroy having been advertised that some troops had appeared in a hostile manner on the frontiers, went against them. I parted from him, and arrived at Fremona, where the Portuguese expected me with great impatience. I reposited the bones of Don Christopher de Gama in a decent place, and sent them the May following to the viceroy of the Indies, together with his arms, which had been presented me by a gentleman of Abyssinia, and a picture of the Virgin Mary, which that gallant Portuguese always carried about him.

The viceroy, during all the time he was engaged in this expedition, heard very provoking accounts of the bad conduct of his wife, and complained of it to the Emperor, entreating him either to punish his daughter himself, or to permit him to deliver her over to justice, that, if she was falsely accused, she might have an opportunity of putting her own honour and her husband's out of dispute. The Emperor took little notice of his son-in-law's remonstrances; and, the truth is, the viceroy was somewhat more nice in that matter than the people of rank in this country generally are. There are laws, it is true, against adultery, but they seem to have been only for the meaner people, and the women of quality, especially the ouzoros, or ladies of the blood royal, are so much above them, that their husbands have not even the liberty of complaining; and certainly to support injuries of this kind without complaining requires a degree of patience which few men can boast of. The viceroy's virtue was not proof against this temptation. He fell into a deep melancholy, and resolved to be revenged on his father-in-law. He knew the present temper of the people, that those of the greatest interest and power were by no means pleased with the changes of religion, and only waited for a fair opportunity to revolt; and that these discontents were everywhere heightened by the monks and clergy. Encouraged by these reflections, he was always talking of the just reasons he had to complain of the Emperor, and gave them sufficient room to understand that if they would appear in his party, he would declare himself for the ancient religion, and put himself at the head of those who should take arms in the defence of it. The chief and almost the only thing that hindered him from raising a formidable rebellion, was the mutual distrust they entertained of one another, each fearing that as soon as the Emperor should publish an act of grace, or general amnesty, the greatest part would lay down their arms and embrace it; and this suspicion was imagined more reasonable of the viceroy than of any other. Notwithstanding this difficulty, the priests, who interested themselves much in this revolt, ran with the utmost earnestness from church to church, levelling their sermons against the Emperor and the Catholic religion; and that they might have the better success in putting a stop to all ecclesiastical innovations, they came to a resolution of putting all the missionaries to the sword; and that the viceroy might have no room to hope for a pardon, they obliged him to give the first wound to him that should fall into his hands.

As I was the nearest, and by consequence the most exposed, an order was immediately issued out for apprehending me, it being thought a good expedient to seize me, and force me to build a citadel, into which they might retreat if they should happen to meet with a defeat. The viceroy wrote to me to desire that I would come to him, he having, as he said, an affair of the highest importance to communicate.

The frequent assemblies which the viceroy held had already been much talked of; and I had received advice that he was ready for a revolt, and that my death was to be the first signal of an open war. Knowing that the viceroy had made many complaints of the treatment he received from his father-in-law, I made no doubt that he had some ill design in hand; and yet could scarce persuade myself that after all the tokens of friendship I had received from him he would enter into any measures for destroying me. While I was yet in suspense, I despatched a faithful servant to the viceroy with my excuse for disobeying him; and gave the messenger strict orders to observe all that passed, and bring me an exact account.

This affair was of too great moment not to engage my utmost endeavours to arrive at the most certain knowledge of it, and to advertise the court of the danger. I wrote, therefore, to one of our fathers, who was then near the Emperor, the best intelligence I could obtain of all that had passed, of the reports that were spread through all this part of the empire, and of the disposition which I discovered in the people to a general defection; telling him, however, that I could not yet believe that the viceroy, who had honoured me with his friendship, and of whom I never had any thought but how to oblige him, could now have so far changed his sentiments as to take away my life.

The letters which I received by my servant, and the assurances he gave that I need fear nothing, for that I was never mentioned by the viceroy without great marks of esteem, so far confirmed me in my error, that I went from Fremona with a resolution to see him. I did not reflect that a man who could fail in his duty to his King, his father-in-law, and his benefactor, might, without scruple, do the same to a stranger, though distinguished as his friend; and thus sanguine and unsuspecting continued my journey, still receiving intimation from all parts to take care of myself. At length, when I was within a few days' journey of the viceroy, I received a billet in more plain and express terms than anything I had been told yet, charging me with extreme imprudence in putting myself into the hands of those men who had undoubtedly sworn to cut me off.

I began, upon this, to distrust the sincerity of the viceroy's professions, and resolved, upon the receipt of another letter from the viceroy, to return directly. In this letter, having excused himself for not waiting for my arrival, he desired me in terms very strong and pressing to come forward, and stay for him at his own house, assuring me that he had given such orders for my entertainment as should prevent my being tired with living there. I imagined at first that he had left some servants to provide for my reception, but being advertised at the same time that there was no longer any doubt of the certainty of his revolt, that the Galles were engaged to come to his assistance, and that he was gone to sign a treaty with them, I was no longer in suspense what measures to take, but returned to Fremona.

Here I found a letter from the Emperor, which prohibited me to go out, and the orders which he had sent through all these parts, directing them to arrest me wherever I was found, and to hinder me from proceeding on my journey. These orders came too late to contribute to my preservation, and this prince's goodness had been in vain, if God, whose protection I have often had experience of in my travels, had not been my conductor in this emergency.

The viceroy, hearing that I was returned to my residence, did not discover any concern or chagrin as at a disappointment, for such was his privacy and dissimulation that the most penetrating could never form any conjecture that could be depended on, about his designs, till everything was ready for the execution of them. My servant, a man of wit, was surprised as well as everybody else; and I can ascribe to nothing but a miracle my escape from so many snares as he laid to entrap me.

There happened during this perplexity of my affairs an accident of small consequence in itself, which yet I think deserves to be mentioned, as it shows the credulity and ignorance of the Abyssins. I received a visit from a religious, who passed, though he was blind, for the most learned person in all that country. He had the whole Scriptures in his memory, but seemed to have been at more pains to retain them than understand them; as he talked much he often took occasion to quote them, and did it almost always improperly. Having invited him to sup and pass the night with me, I set before him some excellent mead, which he liked so well as to drink somewhat beyond the bounds of exact temperance. Next day, to make some return for his entertainment, he took upon him to divert me with some of those stories which the monks amuse simple people with, and told me of a devil that haunted a fountain, and used to make it his employment to plague the monks that came thither to fetch water, and continued his malice till he was converted by the founder of their order, who found him no very stubborn proselyte till they came to the point of circumcision; the devil was unhappily prepossessed with a strong aversion from being circumcised, which, however, by much persuasion, he at last agreed to, and afterwards taking a religious habit, died ten years after with great signs of sanctity. He added another history of a famous Abyssinian monk, who killed a devil two hundred feet high, and only four feet thick, that ravaged all the country; the peasants had a great desire to throw the dead carcase from the top of a rock, but could not with all their force remove it from the place, but the monk drew it after him with all imaginable ease and pushed it down. This story was followed by another, of a young devil that became a religious of the famous monastery of Aba Gatima. The good father would have favoured me with more relations of the same kind, if I had been in the humour to have heard them, but, interrupting him, I told him that all these relations confirmed what we had found by experience, that the monks of Abyssinia were no improper company for the devil.

CHAPTER IX

The viceroy is defeated and hanged. The author narrowly escapes being poisoned.

I did not stay long at Fremona, but left that town and the province of Tigre, and soon found that I was very happy in that resolution, for scarce had I left the place before the viceroy came in person to put me to death, who, not finding me, as he expected, resolved to turn all his vengeance against the father Gaspard Paes, a venerable man, who was grown grey in the missions of Fthiopia, and five other missionaries newly arrived from the Indies; his design was to kill them all at one time without suffering any to escape; he therefore sent for them all, but one happily being sick, another stayed to attend him; to this they owed their lives, for the viceroy, finding but four of them, sent them back, telling them he would see them all together. The fathers, having been already told of his revolt, and of the pretences he made use of to give it credit, made no question of his intent to massacre them, and contrived their escape so that they got safely out of his power.

The viceroy, disappointed in his scheme, vented all his rage upon Father James, whom the patriarch had given him as his confessor; the good man was carried, bound hand and foot, into the middle of the camp; the viceroy gave the first stab in the throat, and all the rest struck him with their lances, and dipped their weapons in his blood, promising each other that they would never accept of any act of oblivion or terms of peace by which the Catholic religion was not abolished throughout the empire, and all those who professed it either banished or put to death. They then ordered all the beads, images, crosses, and relics which the Catholics made use of to be thrown into the fire.

The anger of God was now ready to fall upon his head for these daring and complicated crimes; the Emperor had already confiscated all his goods, and given the government of the kingdom of Tigre to Keba Christos, a good Catholic, who was sent with a numerous army to take possession of it. As both armies were in search of each other, it was not long before they came to a battle. The revolted viceroy Tecla Georgis placed all his confidence in the Galles, his auxiliaries. Keba Christos, who had marched with incredible expedition to hinder the enemy from making any intrenchments, would willingly have refreshed his men a few days before the battle, but finding the foe vigilant, thought it not proper to stay till he was attacked, and therefore resolved to make the first onset; then presenting himself before his army without arms and with his head uncovered, assured them that such was his confidence in God's protection of those that engaged in so just a cause, that though he were in that condition and alone, he would attack his enemies.

The battle began immediately, and of all the troops of Tecla Georgis only the Galles made any resistance, the rest abandoned him without striking a blow. The unhappy commander, seeing all his squadrons broken, and three hundred of the Galles, with twelve ecclesiastics, killed on the spot, hid himself in a cave, where he was found three days afterwards, with his favourite and a monk. When they took him, they cut off the heads of his two companions in the field, and carried him to the Emperor; the procedure against him was not long, and he was condemned to be burnt alive. Then imagining that, if he embraced the Catholic faith, the intercession of the missionaries, with the entreaties of his wife and children, might procure him a pardon, he desired a Jesuit to hear his confession, and abjured his errors. The Emperor was inflexible both to the entreaties of his daughter and the tears of his grand-children, and all that could be obtained of him was that the sentence should be mollified, and changed into a condemnation to be hanged. Tecla Georgis renounced his abjuration, and at his death persisted in his errors. Adero, his sister, who had borne the greatest share in his revolt, was hanged on the same tree fifteen days after.

I arrived not long after at the Emperor's court, and had the honour of kissing his hands; but stayed not long in a place where no missionary ought to linger, unless obliged by the most pressing necessity: but being ordered by my superiors into the kingdom of Damote, I set out on my journey, and on the road was in great danger of losing my life by my curiosity of tasting a herb, which I found near a brook, and which, though I had often heard of it, I did not know. It bears a great resemblance to our radishes; the leaf and colour were beautiful, and the taste not unpleasant. It came into my mind when I began to chew it that perhaps it might be that venomous herb against which no antidote had yet been found, but persuading myself afterwards that my fears were merely chimerical, I continued to chew it, till a man accidentally meeting me, and seeing me with a handful of it, cried out to me that I was poisoned; I had happily not swallowed any of it, and throwing out what I had in my mouth, I returned God thanks for this instance of his protection.

I crossed the Nile the first time in my journey to the kingdom of Damote; my passage brought into my mind all that I had read either in ancient or modern writers of this celebrated river; I recollected the great expenses at which some Emperors had endeavoured to gratify their curiosity of knowing the sources of this mighty stream, which nothing but their little acquaintance with the Abyssins made so difficult to be found. I passed the river within two days' journey of its head, near a wide plain, which is entirely laid under water when it begins to overflow the banks. Its channel is even here so wide, that a ball-shot from a musket can scarce reach the farther bank. Here is neither boat nor bridge, and the river is so full of hippopotami, or river-horses, and crocodiles, that it is impossible to swim over without danger of being devoured. The only way of passing it is upon floats, which they guide as well as they can with long poles. Nor is even this way without danger, for these destructive animals overturn the floats, and tear the passengers in pieces. The river horse, which lives only on grass and branches of trees, is satisfied with killing the men, but the crocodile being more voracious, feeds upon the carcases.

But since I am arrived at the banks of this renowned river, which I have passed and repassed so many times; and since all that I have read of the nature of its waters, and the causes of its overflowing, is full of fables, the reader may not be displeased to find here an account of what I saw myself, or was told by the inhabitants.

CHAPTER X

A description of the Nile.

The Nile, which the natives call Abavi, that is, the Father of Waters, rises first in Sacala, a province of the kingdom of Goiama, which is one of the most fruitful and agreeable of all the Abyssinian dominions. This province is inhabited by a nation of the Agaus, who call, but only call, themselves Christians, for by daily intermarriages they have allied themselves to the Pagan Agaus, and adopted all their customs and ceremonies. These two nations are very numerous, fierce, and unconquerable, inhabiting a country full of mountains, which are covered with woods, and hollowed by nature into vast caverns, many of which are capable of containing several numerous families, and hundreds of cows. To these recesses the Agaus betake themselves when they are driven out of the plain, where it is almost impossible to find them, and certain ruin to pursue them. This people increases extremely, every man being allowed so many wives as he hath hundreds of cows, and it is seldom that the hundreds are required to be complete.

In the eastern part of this kingdom, on the declivity of a mountain, whose descent is so easy that it seems a beautiful plain, is that source of the Nile which has been sought after at so much expense of labour, and about which such variety of conjectures hath been formed without success. This spring, or rather these two springs, are two holes, each about two feet diameter, a stone's cast distant from each other; the one is but about five feet and a half in depth—at least we could not get our plummet farther, perhaps because it was stopped by roots, for the whole place is full of trees; of the other, which is somewhat less, with a line of ten feet we could find no bottom, and were assured by the inhabitants that none ever had been found. It is believed here that these springs are the vents of a great subterraneous lake, and they have this circumstance to favour their opinion, that the ground is always moist and so soft that the water boils up under foot as one walks upon it. This is more visible after rains, for then the ground yields and sinks so much, that I believe it is chiefly supported by the roots of trees that are interwoven one with another; such is the ground round about these fountains. At a little distance to the south is a village named Guix, through which the way lies to the top of the mountain, from whence the traveller discovers a vast extent of land, which appears like a deep valley, though the mountain rises so imperceptibly that those who go up or down it are scarce sensible of any declivity.

On the top of this mountain is a little hill which the idolatrous Agaus have in great veneration; their priest calls them together at this place once a year, and having sacrificed a cow, throws the head into one of the springs of the Nile; after which ceremony, every one sacrifices a cow or more, according to their different degrees of wealth or devotion. The bones of these cows have already formed two mountains of considerable height, which afford a sufficient proof that these nations have always paid their adorations to this famous river. They eat these sacrifices with great devotion, as flesh consecrated to their deity. Then the priest anoints himself with the grease and tallow of the cows, and sits down on a heap of straw, on the top and in the middle of a pile which is prepared; they set fire to it, and the whole heap is consumed without any injury to the priest, who while the fire continues harangues the standers by, and confirms them in their present ignorance and superstition. When the pile is burnt, and the discourse at an end, every one makes a large present to the priest, which is the grand design of this religious mockery.

To return to the course of the Nile: its waters, after the first rise, run to the eastward for about a musket-shot, then turning to the north, continue hidden in the grass and weeds for about a quarter of a league, and discover themselves for the first time among some rocks—a sight not to be enjoyed without some pleasure by those who have read the fabulous accounts of this stream delivered by the ancients, and the vain conjectures and reasonings which have been formed upon its original, the nature of its water, its cataracts, and its inundations, all which we are now entirely acquainted with and eye-witnesses of.

Many interpreters of the Holy Scriptures pretend that Gihon, mentioned in Genesis, is no other than the Nile, which encompasseth all Fthiopia; but as the Gihon had its source from the terrestrial paradise, and we know that the Nile rises in the country of the Agaus, it will be found, I believe, no small difficulty to conceive how the same river could arise from two sources so distant from each other, or how a river from so low a source should spring up and appear in a place perhaps the highest in the world: for if we consider that Arabia and Palestine are in their situation almost level with Egypt; that Egypt is as low, if compared with the kingdom of Dambia, as the deepest valley in regard of the highest mountain; that the province of Sacala is yet more elevated than Dambia; that the waters of the Nile must either pass under the Red Sea, or take a great compass about, we shall find it hard to conceive such an attractive power in the earth as may be able to make the waters rise through the obstruction of so much sand from places so low to the most lofty region of Fthiopia.

But leaving these difficulties, let us go on to describe the course of the Nile. It rolls away from its source with so inconsiderable a current, that it appears unlikely to escape being dried up by the hot season, but soon receiving an increase from the Gemma, the Keltu, the Bransu, and other less rivers, it is of such a breadth in the plain of Boad, which is not above three days' journey from its source, that a ball shot from a musket will scarce fly from one bank to the other. Here it begins to run northwards, deflecting, however, a little towards the east, for the space of nine or ten leagues, and then enters the so much talked of Lake of Dambia, called by the natives Bahar Sena, the Resemblance of the Sea, or Bahar Dambia, the Sea of Dambia. It crosses this lake only at one end with so violent a rapidity, that the waters of the Nile may be distinguished through all the passage, which is six leagues. Here begins the greatness of the Nile. Fifteen miles farther, in the land of Alata, it rushes precipitately from the top of a high rock, and forms one of the most beautiful water-falls in the world: I passed under it without being wet; and resting myself there, for the sake of the coolness, was charmed with a thousand delightful rainbows, which the sunbeams painted on the water in all their shining and lively colours. The fall of this mighty stream from so great a height makes a noise that may be heard to a considerable distance; but I could not observe that the neighbouring inhabitants were at all deaf. I conversed with several, and was as easily heard by them as I heard them. The mist that rises from this fall of water may be seen much farther than the noise can be heard. After this cataract the Nile again collects its scattered stream among the rocks, which seem to be disjoined in this place only to afford it a passage. They are so near each other that, in my time, a bridge of beams, on which the whole Imperial army passed, was laid over them. Sultan Segued hath since built here a bridge of one arch in the same place, for which purpose he procured masons from India. This bridge, which is the first the Abyssins have seen on the Nile, very much facilitates a communication between the provinces, and encourages commerce among the inhabitants of his empire.

Here the river alters its course, and passes through many various kingdoms; on the east it leaves Begmeder, or the Land of Sheep, so called from great numbers that are bred there, beg, in that language, signifying sheep, and meder, a country. It then waters the kingdoms of Amhara, Olaca, Choaa, and Damot, which lie on the left side, and the kingdom of Goiama, which it bounds on the right, forming by its windings a kind of peninsula. Then entering Bezamo, a province of the kingdom of Damot, and Gamarchausa, part of Goiama, it returns within a short day's journey of its spring; though to pursue it through all its mazes, and accompany it round the kingdom of Goiama, is a journey of twenty-nine days. So far, and a few days' journey farther, this river confines itself to Abyssinia, and then passes into the bordering countries of Fazulo and Ombarca.

These vast regions we have little knowledge of: they are inhabited by nations entirely different from the Abyssins; their hair is like that of the other blacks, short and curled. In the year 1615, Rassela Christos, lieutenant-general to Sultan Segued, entered those kingdoms with his army in a hostile manner; but being able to get no intelligence of the condition of the people, and astonished at their unbounded extent, he returned, without daring to attempt anything.

As the empire of the Abyssins terminates at these deserts, and as I have followed the course of the Nile no farther, I here leave it to range over barbarous kingdoms, and convey wealth and plenty into Egypt, which owes to the annual inundations of this river its envied fertility. I know not anything of the rest of its passage, but that it receives great increases from many other rivers; that it has several cataracts like the first already described, and that few fish are to be found in it, which scarcity, doubtless, is to be attributed to the river-horses and crocodiles, which destroy the weaker inhabitants of these waters, and something may be allowed to the cataracts, it being difficult for fish to fall so far without being killed.

Although some who have travelled in Asia and Africa have given the world their descriptions of crocodiles and hippopotamus, or river-horse, yet as the Nile has at least as great numbers of each as any river in the world, I cannot but think my account of it would be imperfect without some particular mention of these animals.

The crocodile is very ugly, having no proportion between his length and thickness; he hath short feet, a wide mouth, with two rows of sharp teeth, standing wide from each other, a brown skin so fortified with scales, even to his nose, that a musket-ball cannot penetrate it. His sight is extremely quick, and at a great distance. In the water he is daring and fierce, and will seize on any that are so unfortunate as to be found by him bathing, who, if they escape with life, are almost sure to leave some limb in his mouth. Neither I, nor any with whom I have conversed about the crocodile, have ever seen him weep, and therefore I take the liberty of ranking all that hath been told us of his tears amongst the fables which are only proper to amuse children.

The hippopotamus, or river-horse, grazes upon the land and browses on the shrubs, yet is no less dangerous than the crocodile. He is the size of an ox, of a brown colour without any hair, his tail is short, his neck long, and his head of an enormous bigness; his eyes are small, his mouth wide, with teeth half a foot long; he hath two tusks like those of a wild boar, but larger; his legs are short, and his feet part into four toes. It is easy to observe from this description that he hath no resemblance of a horse, and indeed nothing could give occasion to the name but some likeness in his ears, and his neighing and snorting like a horse when he is provoked or raises his head out of water. His hide is so hard that a musket fired close to him can only make a slight impression, and the best tempered lances pushed forcibly against him are either blunted or shivered, unless the assailant has the skill to make his thrust at certain parts which are more tender. There is great danger in meeting him, and the best way is, upon such an accident, to step aside and let him pass by. The flesh of this animal doth not differ from that of a cow, except that it is blacker and harder to digest.

The ignorance which we have hitherto been in of the original of the Nile hath given many authors an opportunity of presenting us very gravely with their various systems and conjectures about the nature of its waters, and the reason of its overflows.

It is easy to observe how many empty hypotheses and idle reasonings the phenomena of this river have put mankind to the expense of. Yet there are people so bigoted to antiquity, as not to pay any regard to the relation of travellers who have been upon the spot, and by the evidence of their eyes can confute all that the ancients have written. It was difficult, it was even impossible, to arrive at the source of the Nile by tracing its channel from the mouth; and all who ever attempted it, having been stopped by the cataracts, and imagining none that followed them could pass farther, have taken the liberty of entertaining us with their own fictions.

It is to be remembered likewise that neither the Greeks nor Romans, from whom we have received all our information, ever carried their arms into this part of the world, or ever heard of multitudes of nations that dwell upon the banks of this vast river; that the countries where the Nile rises, and those through which it runs, have no inhabitants but what are savage and uncivilised; that before they could arrive at its head, they must surmount the insuperable obstacles of impassable forests, inaccessible cliffs, and deserts crowded with beasts of prey, fierce by nature, and raging for want of sustenance. Yet if they who endeavoured with so much ardour to discover the spring of this river had landed at Mazna on the coast of the Red Sea, and marched a little more to the south than the southwest, they might perhaps have gratified their curiosity at less expense, and in about twenty days might have enjoyed the desired sight of the sources of the Nile.

But this discovery was reserved for the invincible bravery of our noble countrymen, who, not discouraged by the dangers of a navigation in seas never explored before, have subdued kingdoms and empires where the Greek and Roman greatness, where the names of Cfsar and Alexander, were never heard of; who have demolished the airy fabrics of renowned hypotheses, and detected those fables which the ancients rather chose to invent of the sources of the Nile than to confess their ignorance. I cannot help suspending my narration to reflect a little on the ridiculous speculations of those swelling philosophers, whose arrogance would prescribe laws to nature, and subject those astonishing effects, which we behold daily, to their idle reasonings and chimerical rules. Presumptuous imagination! that has given being to such numbers of books, and patrons to so many various opinions about the overflows of the Nile. Some of these theorists have been pleased to declare it as their favourite notion that this inundation is caused by high winds which stop the current, and so force the water to rise above its banks, and spread over all Egypt. Others pretend a subterraneous communication between the ocean and the Nile, and that the sea being violently agitated swells the river. Many have imagined themselves blessed with the discovery when they have told us that this mighty flood proceeds from the melting of snow on the mountains of Fthiopia, without reflecting that this opinion is contrary to the received notion of all the ancients, who believed that the heat was so excessive between the tropics that no inhabitant could live there. So much snow and so great heat are never met with in the same region; and indeed I never saw snow in Abyssinia, except on Mount Semen in the kingdom of Tigre, very remote from the Nile, and on Namera, which is indeed not far distant, but where there never falls snow sufficient to wet the foot of the mountain when it is melted.

To the immense labours and fatigues of the Portuguese mankind is indebted for the knowledge of the real cause of these inundations so great and so regular. Their observations inform us that Abyssinia, where the Nile rises and waters vast tracts of land, is full of mountains, and in its natural situation much higher than Egypt; that all the winter, from June to September, no day is without rain; that the Nile receives in its course all the rivers, brooks, and torrents which fall from those mountains; these necessarily swell it above the banks, and fill the plains of Egypt with the inundation. This comes regularly about the month of July, or three weeks after the beginning of a rainy season in Fthiopia. The different degrees of this flood are such certain indications of the fruitfulness or sterility of the ensuing year, that it is publicly proclaimed in Cairo how much the water hath gained each night. This is all I have to inform the reader of concerning the Nile, which the Egyptians adored as the deity, in whose choice it was to bless them with abundance, or deprive them of the necessaries of life.

CHAPTER XI

The author discovers a passage over the Nile. Is sent into the province of Ligonus, which he gives a description of. His success in his mission. The stratagem of the monks to encourage the soldiers. The author narrowly escapes being burned.

When I was to cross this river at Boad, I durst not venture myself on the floats I have already spoken of, but went up higher in hopes of finding a more commodious passage. I had with me three or four men that were reduced to the same difficulty with myself. In one part seeing people on the other side, and remarking that the water was shallow, and that the rocks and trees which grew very thick there contributed to facilitate the attempt, I leaped from one rock to another, till I reached the opposite bank, to the great amazement of the natives themselves, who never had tried that way; my four companions followed me with the same success: and it hath been called since the passage of Father Jerome.

That province of the kingdom of Damot, which I was assigned to by my superior, is called Ligonus, and is perhaps one of the most beautiful and agreeable places in the world; the air is healthful and temperate, and all the mountains, which are not very high, shaded with cedars. They sow and reap here in every season, the ground is always producing, and the fruits ripen throughout the year; so great, so charming is the variety, that the whole region seems a garden laid out and cultivated only to please. I doubt whether even the imagination of a painter has yet conceived a landscape as beautiful as I have seen. The forests have nothing uncouth or savage, and seem only planted for shade and coolness. Among a prodigious number of trees which fill them, there is one kind which I have seen in no other place, and to which we have none that bears any resemblance. This tree, which the natives call ensete, is wonderfully useful; its leaves, which are so large as to cover a man, make hangings for rooms, and serve the inhabitants instead of linen for their tables and carpets. They grind the branches and the thick parts of the leaves, and when they are mingled with milk, find them a delicious food. The trunk and the roots are even more nourishing than the leaves or branches, and the meaner people, when they go a journey, make no provision of any other victuals. The word ensete signifies the tree against hunger, or the poor's tree, though the most wealthy often eat of it. If it be cut down within half a foot of the ground and several incisions made in the stump, each will put out a new sprout, which, if transplanted, will take root and grow to a tree. The Abyssins report that this tree when it is cut down groans like a man, and, on this account, call cutting down an ensete killing it. On the top grows a bunch of five or six figs, of a taste not very agreeable, which they set in the ground to produce more trees.

I stayed two months in the province of Ligonus, and during that time procured a church to be built of hewn stone, roofed and wainscoted with cedar, which is the most considerable in the whole country. My continual employment was the duties of the mission, which I was always practising in some part of the province, not indeed with any extraordinary success at first, for I found the people inflexibly obstinate in their opinions, even to so great a degree, that when I first published the Emperor's edict requiring all his subjects to renounce their errors, and unite themselves to the Roman Church, there were some monks who, to the number of sixty, chose rather to die by throwing themselves headlong from a precipice than obey their sovereign's commands: and in a battle fought between these people that adhered to the religion of their ancestors, and the troops of Sultan Segued, six hundred religious, placing themselves at the head of their men, marched towards the Catholic army with the stones of the altars upon their heads, assuring their credulous followers that the Emperor's troops would immediately at the sight of those stones fall into disorder and turn their backs; but, as they were some of the first that fell, their death had a great influence upon the people to undeceive them, and make them return to the truth. Many were converted after the battle, and when they had embraced the Catholic faith, adhered to that with the same constancy and firmness with which they had before persisted in their errors.

The Emperor had sent a viceroy into this province, whose firm attachment to the Roman Church, as well as great abilities in military affairs, made him a person very capable of executing the orders of the Emperor, and of suppressing any insurrection that might be raised, to prevent those alterations in religion which they were designed to promote: a farther view in the choice of so warlike a deputy was that a stop might be put to the inroads of the Galles, who had killed one viceroy, and in a little time after killed this.

It was our custom to meet together every year about Christmas, not only that we might comfort and entertain each other, but likewise that we might relate the progress and success of our missions, and concert all measures that might farther the conversion of the inhabitants. This year our place of meeting was the Emperor's camp, where the patriarch and superior of the missions were. I left the place of my abode, and took in my way four fathers, that resided at the distance of two days' journey, so that the company, without reckoning our attendants, was five. There happened nothing remarkable to us till the last night of our journey, when taking up our lodging at a place belonging to the Empress, a declared enemy to all Catholics, and in particular to the missionaries, we met with a kind reception in appearance, and were lodged in a large stone house covered with wood and straw, which had stood uninhabited so long, that great numbers of red ants had taken possession of it; these, as soon as we were laid down, attacked us on all sides, and tormented us so incessantly that we were obliged to call up our domestics. Having burnt a prodigious number of these troublesome animals, we tried to compose ourselves again, but had scarce closed our eyes before we were awakened by the fire that had seized our lodging. Our servants, who were fortunately not all gone to bed, perceived the fire as soon as it began, and informed me, who lay nearest the door. I immediately alarmed all the rest, and nothing was thought of but how to save ourselves and the little goods we had, when, to our great astonishment, we found one of the doors barricaded in such a manner that we could not open it. Nothing now could have prevented our perishing in the flames had not those who kindled them omitted to fasten that door near which I was lodged. We were no longer in doubt that the inhabitants of the town had laid a train, and set fire to a neighbouring house, in order to consume us; their measures were so well laid, that the house was in ashes in an instant, and three of our beds were burnt which the violence of the flame would not allow us to carry away. We spent the rest of the night in the most dismal apprehensions, and found next morning that we had justly charged the inhabitants with the design of destroying us, for the place was entirely abandoned, and those that were conscious of the crime had fled from the punishment. We continued our journey, and came to Gorgora, where we found the fathers met, and the Emperor with them.

CHAPTER XII

The author is sent into Tigre. Is in danger of being poisoned by the breath of a serpent. Is stung by a serpent. Is almost killed by eating anchoy. The people conspire against the missionaries, and distress them.

My superiors intended to send me into the farthest parts of the empire, but the Emperor over-ruled that design, and remanded me to Tigre, where I had resided before. I passed in my journey by Ganete Ilhos, a palace newly built, and made agreeable by beautiful gardens, and had the honour of paying my respects to the Emperor, who had retired thither, and receiving from him a large present for the finishing of a hospital, which had been begun in the kingdom of Tigre. After having returned him thanks, I continued my way, and in crossing a desert two days' journey over, was in great danger of my life, for, as I lay on the ground, I perceived myself seized with a pain which forced me to rise, and saw about four yards from me one of those serpents that dart their poison at a distance; although I rose before he came very near me, I yet felt the effects of his poisonous breath, and, if I had lain a little longer, had certainly died; I had recourse to bezoar, a sovereign remedy against these poisons, which I always carried about me. These serpents are not long, but have a body short and thick, and their bellies speckled with brown, black, and yellow; they have a wide mouth, with which they draw in a great quantity of air, and, having retained it some time, eject it with such force that they kill at four yards' distance. I only escaped by being somewhat farther from him. This danger, however, was not much to be regarded in comparison of another which my negligence brought me into. As I was picking up a skin that lay upon the ground, I was stung by a serpent that left his sting in my finger; I at least picked an extraneous substance about the bigness of a hair out of the wound, which I imagined was the sting. This slight wound I took little notice of, till my arm grew inflamed all over; in a short time the poison infected my blood, and I felt the most terrible convulsions, which were interpreted as certain signs that my death was near and inevitable. I received now no benefit from bezoar, the horn of the unicorn, or any of the usual antidotes, but found myself obliged to make use of an extraordinary remedy, which I submitted to with extreme reluctance. This submission and obedience brought the blessing of Heaven upon me; nevertheless, I continued indisposed a long time, and had many symptoms which made me fear that all the danger was not yet over. I then took cloves of garlic, though with a great aversion, both from the taste and smell. I was in this condition a whole month, always in pain, and taking medicines the most nauseous in the world. At length youth and a happy constitution surmounted the malignity, and I recovered my former health.

I continued two years at my residence in Tigre, entirely taken up with the duties of the mission—preaching, confessing, baptising— and enjoyed a longer quiet and repose than I had ever done since I left Portugal. During this time one of our fathers, being always sick and of a constitution which the air of Abyssinia was very hurtful to, obtained a permission from our superiors to return to the Indies; I was willing to accompany him through part of his way, and went with him over a desert, at no great distance from my residence, where I found many trees loaded with a kind of fruit, called by the natives anchoy, about the bigness of an apricot, and very yellow, which is much eaten without any ill effect. I therefore made no scruple of gathering and eating it, without knowing that the inhabitants always peeled it, the rind being a violent purgative; so that, eating the fruit and skin together, I fell into such a disorder as almost brought me to my end. The ordinary dose is six of these rinds, and I had devoured twenty.

I removed from thence to Debaroa, fifty-four miles nearer the sea, and crossed in my way the desert of the province of Saraoe. The country is fruitful, pleasant, and populous; there are greater numbers of Moors in these parts than in any other province of Abyssinia, and the Abyssins of this country are not much better than the Moors.

I was at Debaroa when the prosecution was first set on foot against the Catholics. Sultan Segued, who had been so great a favourer of us, was grown old, and his spirit and authority decreased with his strength. His son, who was arrived at manhood, being weary of waiting so long for the crown he was to inherit, took occasion to blame his father's conduct, and found some reason for censuring all his actions; he even proceeded so far as to give orders sometimes contrary to the Emperor's. He had embraced the Catholic religion, rather through complaisance than conviction or inclination; and many of the Abyssins who had done the same, waited only for an opportunity of making public profession of the ancient erroneous opinions, and of re-uniting themselves to the Church of Alexandria. So artfully can this people dissemble their sentiments that we had not been able hitherto to distinguish our real from our pretended favourers; but as soon as this Prince began to give evident tokens of his hatred, even in the lifetime of the Emperor, we saw all the courtiers and governors who had treated us with such a show of friendship declare against us, and persecute us as disturbers of the public tranquillity, who had come into Fthiopia with no other intention than to abolish the ancient laws and customs of the country, to sow divisions between father and son, and preach up a revolution.

After having borne all sorts of affronts and ill-treatments, we retired to our house at Fremona, in the midst of our countrymen, who had been settling round about us a long time, imagining we should be more secure there, and that, at least during the life of the Emperor, they would not come to extremities, or proceed to open force. I laid some stress upon the kindness which the viceroy of Tigre had shown to us, and in particular to me; but was soon convinced that those hopes had no real foundation, for he was one of the most violent of our persecutors. He seized upon all our lands, and, advancing with his troops to Fremona, blocked up the town. The army had not been stationed there long before they committed all sorts of disorders; so that one day a Portuguese, provoked beyond his temper at the insolence of some of them, went out with his four sons, and, wounding several of them, forced the rest back to their camp.

We thought we had good reason to apprehend an attack; their troops were increasing, our town was surrounded, and on the point of being forced. Our Portuguese therefore thought that, without staying till the last extremities, they might lawfully repel one violence by another, and sallying out to the number of fifty, wounded about three score of the Abyssins, and had put them to the sword but that they feared it might bring too great an odium upon our cause. The Portuguese were some of them wounded, but happily none died on either side.

Though the times were by no means favourable to us, every one blamed the conduct of the viceroy; and those who did not commend our action made the necessity we were reduced to of self-defence an excuse for it. The viceroy's principal design was to get my person into his possession, imagining that if I was once in his power, all the Portuguese would pay him a blind obedience. Having been unsuccessful in his attempt by open force, he made use of the arts of negotiation, but with an event not more to his satisfaction. This viceroy being recalled, a son-in-law of the Emperor's succeeded, who treated us even worse than his predecessor had done.

When he entered upon his command, he loaded us with kindnesses, giving us so many assurances of his protection that, while the Emperor lived, we thought him one of our friends; but no sooner was our protector dead than this man pulled off his mask, and, quitting all shame, let us see that neither the fear of God nor any other consideration was capable of restraining him when we were to be distressed. The persecution then becoming general, there was no longer any place of security for us in Abyssinia, where we were looked upon by all as the authors of all the civil commotions, and many councils were held to determine in what manner they should dispose of us. Several were of opinion that the best way would be to kill us all at once, and affirmed that no other means were left of re-establishing order and tranquillity in the kingdom.

Others, more prudent, were not for putting us to death with so little consideration, but advised that we should be banished to one of the isles of the Lake of Dambia, an affliction more severe than death itself. These alleged in vindication of their opinions that it was reasonable to expect, if they put us to death, that the viceroy of the Indies would come with fire and sword to demand satisfaction. This argument made so great an impression upon some of them that they thought no better measures could be taken than to send us back again to the Indies. This proposal, however, was not without its difficulties, for they suspected that when we should arrive at the

Portuguese territories, we would levy an army, return back to Abyssinia, and under pretence of establishing the Catholic religion revenge all the injuries we had suffered. While they were thus deliberating upon our fate, we were imploring the succour of the Almighty with fervent and humble supplications, entreating him in the midst of our sighs and tears that he would not suffer his own cause to miscarry, and that, however it might please him to dispose of our lives — which, we prayed, he would assist us to lay down with patience and resignation worthy of the faith for which we were persecuted — he would not permit our enemies to triumph over the truth.

Thus we passed our days and nights in prayers, in affliction, and tears, continually crowded with widows and orphans that subsisted upon our charity and came to us for bread when we had not any for ourselves.

While we were in this distress we received an account that the viceroy of the Indies had fitted out a powerful fleet against the King of Mombaza, who, having thrown off the authority of the Portuguese, had killed the governor of the fortress, and had since committed many acts of cruelty. The same fleet, as we were informed, after the King of Mombaza was reduced, was to burn and ruin Zeila, in revenge of the death of two Portuguese Jesuits who were killed by the King in the year 1604. As Zeila was not far from the frontiers of Abyssinia, they imagined that they already saw the Portuguese invading their country.

The viceroy of Tigre had inquired of me a few days before how many men one India ship carried, and being told that the complement of some was a thousand men, he compared that answer with the report then spread over all the country, that there were eighteen Portuguese vessels on the coast of Adel, and concluded that they were manned by an army of eighteen thousand men; then considering what had been achieved by four hundred, under the command of Don Christopher de Gama, he thought Abyssinia already ravaged, or subjected to the King of Portugal. Many declared themselves of his opinion, and the court took its measures with respect to us from these uncertain and ungrounded rumours. Some were so infatuated with their apprehensions that they undertook to describe the camp of the Portuguese, and affirmed that they had heard the report of their cannons.

All this contributed to exasperate the inhabitants, and reduced us often to the point of being massacred. At length they came to a resolution of giving us up to the Turks, assuring them that we were masters of a vast treasure, in hope that after they had inflicted all kinds of tortures on us, to make us confess where we had hid our gold, or what we had done with it, they would at length kill us in rage for the disappointment. Nor was this their only view, for they believed that the Turks would, by killing us, kindle such an irreconcilable hatred between themselves and our nation as would make it necessary for them to keep us out of the Red Sea, of which they are entirely masters: so that their determination was as politic as cruel. Some pretend that the Turks were engaged to put us to death as soon as we were in their power.

CHAPTER XIII

The author relieves the patriarch and missionaries, and supports them. He escapes several snares laid for him by the viceroy of Tigre. They put themselves under the protection of the Prince of Bar.

Having concluded this negotiation, they drove us out of our houses, and robbed us of everything that was worth carrying away; and, not content with that, informed some banditti that were then in those parts of the road we were to travel through, so that the patriarch and some missionaries were attacked in a desert by these rovers, with their captain at their head, who pillaged his library, his ornaments, and what little baggage the missionaries had left, and might have gone away without resistance or interruption had they satisfied themselves with only robbing; but when they began to fall upon the missionaries and their companions, our countrymen, finding that their lives could only be preserved by their courage, charged their enemies with such vigour that they killed their chief and forced the rest to a precipitate flight. But these rovers, being acquainted with the country, harassed the little caravan till it was past the borders.

Our fathers then imagined they had nothing more to fear, but too soon were convinced of their error, for they found the whole country turned against them, and met everywhere new enemies to contend with and new dangers to surmount. Being not far distant from Fremona, where I resided, they sent to me for succour. I was better informed of the distress they were in than themselves, having been told that a numerous body of Abyssins had posted themselves in a narrow pass with an intent to surround and destroy them; therefore, without long deliberation, I assembled my friends, both Portuguese and Abyssins, to the number of fourscore, and went to their rescue, carrying with me provisions and refreshments, of which I knew they were in great need. These glorious confessors I met as they were just entering the pass designed for the place of their destruction, and doubly preserved them from famine and the sword. A grateful sense of their deliverance made them receive me as a guardian angel. We went together to Fremona, and being in all a patriarch, a bishop, eighteen Jesuits, and four hundred Portuguese whom I supplied with necessaries, though the revenues of our house were lost, and though the country was disaffected to us, in the worst season of the year. We were obliged for the relief of the poor and our own subsistence to sell our ornaments and chalices, which we first broke in pieces, that the people might not have the pleasure of ridiculing our mysteries by profaning the vessels made use of in the celebration of them, for they now would gladly treat with the highest indignities what they had a year before looked upon with veneration.

Amidst all these perplexities the viceroy did not fail to visit us, and make us great offers of service in expectation of a large present. We were in a situation in which it was very difficult to act properly; we knew too well the ill intentions of the viceroy, but durst not complain, or give him any reason to imagine that we knew them. We longed to retreat out of his power, or at least to send one of our company to the Indies with an account of persecution we suffered, and could without his leave neither do one nor the other.

When it was determined that one should be sent to the Indies, I was at first singled out for the journey, and it was intended that I should represent at Goa, at Rome, and at Madrid the distresses and necessities of the mission of Fthiopia; but the fathers reflecting afterwards that I best understood the Abyssinian language, and was most acquainted with the customs of the country, altered their opinions, and, continuing me in Fthiopia either to perish with them or preserve them, deputed four other Jesuits, who in a short time set out on their way to the Indies.

About this time I was sent for to the viceroy's camp to confess a criminal, who, though falsely, was believed a Catholic, to whom, after a proper exhortation, I was going to pronounce the form of absolution, when those that waited to execute him told him aloud that if he expected to save his life by professing himself a Catholic, he would find himself deceived, and that he had nothing to do but prepare himself for death. The unhappy criminal had no sooner heard this than, rising up, he declared his resolution to die in the religion of his country, and being delivered up to his prosecutors was immediately dispatched with their lances.

The chief reason of calling me was not that I might hear this confession: the viceroy had another design of seizing my person, expecting that either the Jesuits or Portuguese would buy my liberty with a large ransom, or that he might exchange me for his father, who was kept prisoner by a revolted prince. That prince would have been no loser by the exchange, for so much was I hated by the Abyssinian monks that they would have thought no expense too great to have gotten me into their hands, that they might have glutted their revenge by putting me to the most painful death they could have invented. Happily I found means to retire out of this dangerous place, and was followed by the viceroy almost to Fremona, who, being disappointed, desired me either to visit him at his camp, or appoint a place where we might confer. I made many excuses, but at length agreed to meet him at a place near Fremona, bringing each of us only three companions. I did not doubt but he would bring more, and so he did, but found that I was upon my guard, and that my company increased in proportion to his. My friends were resolute Portuguese, who were determined to give him no quarter if he made any attempt upon my liberty. Finding himself once more countermined, he returned ashamed to his camp, where a month after, being accused of a confederacy in the revolt of that prince who kept his father prisoner, he was arrested, and carried in chains to the Emperor.

The time now approaching in which we were to be delivered to the Turks, we had none but God to apply to for relief: all the measures we could think of were equally dangerous. Resolving, nevertheless, to seek some retreat where we might hide ourselves either all together or separately, we determined at last to put ourselves under the protection of the Prince John Akay, who had defended himself a long time in the province of Bar against the power of Abyssinia.

After I had concluded a treaty with this prince, the patriarch and all the fathers put themselves into his hands, and being received with all imaginable kindness and civility, were conducted with a guard to Adicota, a rock excessively steep, about nine miles from his place of residence. The event was not agreeable to the happy beginning of our negotiation, for we soon began to find that our habitation was not likely to be very pleasant. We were surrounded with Mahometans, or Christians who were inveterate enemies to the Catholic faith, and were obliged to act with the utmost caution. Notwithstanding these inconveniences we were pleased with the present tranquillity we enjoyed, and lived contentedly on lentils and a little corn that we had; and I, after we had sold all our goods, resolved to turn physician, and was soon able to support myself by my practice.

I was once consulted by a man troubled with asthma, who presented me with two alquieres—that is, about twenty-eight pounds weight—of corn and a sheep. The advice I gave him, after having turned over my books, was to drink goats' urine every morning; I know not whether he found any benefit by following my prescription, for I never saw him after.

Being under a necessity of obeying our acoba, or protector, we changed our place of abode as often as he desired it, though not without great inconveniences, from the excessive heat of the weather and the faintness which our strict observation of the fasts and austerities of Lent, as it is kept in this country, had brought upon us. At length, wearied with removing so often, and finding that the last place assigned for our abode was always the worst, we agreed that I should go to our sovereign and complain.

I found him entirely taken up with the imagination of a prodigious treasure, affirmed by the monks to be hidden under a mountain. He was told that his predecessors had been hindered from discovering it by the demon that guarded it, but that the demon was now at a great distance from his charge, and was grown blind and lame; that having lost his son, and being without any children except a daughter that was ugly and unhealthy, he was under great affliction, and entirely neglected the care of his treasure; that if he should come, they could call one of their ancient brothers to their assistance, who, being a man of a most holy life, would be able to prevent his making any resistance. To all these stories the prince listened with unthinking credulity. The monks, encouraged by this, fell to the business, and brought a man above a hundred years old, whom, because he could not support himself on horseback, they had tied on the beast, and covered him with black wool. He was followed by a black cow (designed for a sacrifice to the demon of the place), and by some monks that carried mead, beer, and parched corn, to complete the offering.

No sooner were they arrived at the foot of the mountain than every one began to work: bags were brought from all parts to convey away the millions which each imagined would be his share. The Xumo, who superintended the work, would not allow any one to come near the labourers, but stood by, attended by the old monk, who almost sang himself to death. At length, having removed a vast quantity of earth and stones, they discovered some holes made by rats or moles, at sight of which a shout of joy ran through the whole troop: the cow was brought and sacrificed immediately, and some pieces of flesh were thrown into these holes. Animated now with assurance of success, they lose no time: every one redoubles his endeavours, and the heat, though intolerable, was less powerful than the hopes they had conceived. At length some, not so patient as the rest, were weary, and desisted. The work now grew more difficult; they found nothing but rock, yet continued to toil on, till the prince, having lost all temper, began to inquire with some passion when he should have a sight of this treasure, and after having been some time amused with many promises by the monks, was told that he had not faith enough to be favoured with the discovery.

All this I saw myself, and could not forbear endeavouring to convince our protector how much he was imposed upon: he was not long before he was satisfied that he had been too credulous, for all those that had so industriously searched after this imaginary wealth, within five hours left the work in despair, and I continued almost alone with the prince.

Imagining no time more proper to make the proposal I was sent with than while his passion was still hot against the monks, I presented him with two ounces of gold and two plates of silver, with some other things of small value, and was so successful that he gratified me in all my requests, and gave us leave to return to Adicora, where we were so fortunate to find our huts yet uninjured and entire.

About this time the fathers who had stayed behind at Fremona arrived with the new viceroy, and an officer fierce in the defence of his own religion, who had particular orders to deliver all the Jesuits up to the Turks, except me, whom the Emperor was resolved to have in his own hands, alive or dead. We had received some notice of this resolution from our friends at court, and were likewise informed that the Emperor, their master, had been persuaded that my design was to procure assistance from the Indies, and that I should certainly return at the head of an army. The patriarch's advice upon this emergency was that I should retire into the woods, and by some other road join the nine Jesuits who were gone towards Mazna. I could think of no better expedient, and therefore went away in the night between the 23rd and 24th of April with my comrade, an old man, very infirm and very timorous. We crossed woods never crossed, I believe, by any before: the darkness of the night and the thickness of the shade spread a kind of horror round us; our gloomy journey was still more incommoded by the brambles and thorns, which tore our hands; amidst all these difficulties I applied myself to the Almighty, praying him to preserve us from those dangers which we endeavoured to avoid, and to deliver us from those to which our flight exposed us. Thus we travelled all night, till eight next morning, without taking either rest or food; then, imagining ourselves secure, we made us some cakes of barley-meal and water, which we thought a feast.

We had a dispute with our guides, who though they had bargained to conduct us for an ounce of gold, yet when they saw us so entangled in the intricacies of the wood that we could not possibly get out without their direction, demanded seven ounces of gold, a mule, and a little tent which we had; after a long dispute we were forced to come to their terms. We continued to travel all night, and to hide ourselves in the woods all day: and here it was that we met the three hundred elephants I spoke of before. We made long marches, travelling without any halt from four in the afternoon to eight in the morning.

Arriving at a valley where travellers seldom escape being plundered, we were obliged to double our pace, and were so happy as to pass it without meeting with any misfortune, except that we heard a bird sing on our left hand — a certain presage among these people of some great calamity at hand. As there is no reasoning them out of superstition, I knew no way of encouraging them to go forward but what I had already made use of on the same occasion, assuring them that I heard one at the same time on the right. They were happily so credulous as to take my word, and we went on till we came to a well, where we stayed awhile to refresh ourselves. Setting out again in the evening, we passed so near a village where these robbers had retreated that the dogs barked after us. Next morning we joined the fathers, who waited for us. After we had rested ourselves some time in that mountain, we resolved to separate and go two and two, to seek for a more convenient place where we might hide ourselves. We had not gone far before we were surrounded by a troop of robbers, with whom, by the interest of some of the natives who had joined themselves to our caravan, we came to a composition, giving them part of our goods to permit us to carry away the rest; and after this troublesome adventure arrived at a place something more commodious than that which we had quitted, where we met with bread, but of so pernicious a quality that, after having ate it, we were intoxicated to so great a degree that one of my friends, seeing me so disordered, congratulated my good fortune of having met with such good wine, and was surprised when I gave him an account of the whole affair. He then offered me some curdled milk, very sour, with barley-meal, which we boiled, and thought it the best entertainment we had met with a long time.

CHAPTER XIV

They are betrayed into the hands of the Turks; are detained awhile at Mazna; are threatened by the Bassa of Suaquem. They agree for their ransom, and are part of them dismissed.

Some time after, we received news that we should prepare ourselves to serve the Turks—a message which filled us with surprise, it having never been known that one of these lords had ever abandoned any whom he had taken under his protection; and it is, on the contrary, one of the highest points of honour amongst them to risk their fortunes and their lives in the defence of their dependants who have implored their protection. But neither law nor justice was of any advantage to us, and the customs of the country were doomed to be broken when they would have contributed to our security.

We were obliged to march in the extremity of the hot season, and had certainly perished by the fatigue had we not entered the woods, which shaded us from the scorching sun. The day before our arrival at the place where we were to be delivered to the Turks, we met with five elephants, that pursued us, and if they could have come to us would have prevented the miseries we afterwards endured, but God had decreed otherwise.

On the morrow we came to the banks of a river, where we found fourscore Turks that waited for us, armed with muskets. They let us rest awhile, and then put us into the hands of our new masters, who, setting us upon camels, conducted us to Mazna. Their commander, seeming to be touched with our misfortunes, treated us with much gentleness and humanity; he offered us coffee, which we drank, but with little relish. We came next day to Mazna, in so wretched a condition that we were not surprised at being hooted by the boys, but thought ourselves well used that they threw no stones at us.

As soon as we were brought hither, all we had was taken from us, and we were carried to the governor, who is placed there by the Bassa of Suaquem. Having been told by the Abyssins that we had carried all the gold out of Fthiopia, they searched us with great exactness, but found nothing except two chalices, and some relics of so little value that we redeemed them for six sequins. As I had given them my chalice upon their first demand, they did not search me, but gave us to understand that they expected to find something of greater value, which either we must have hidden or the Abyssins must have imposed on them. They left us the rest of the day at a gentleman's house, who was our friend, from whence the next day they fetched us to transport us to the island, where they put us into a kind of prison, with a view of terrifying us into a confession of the place where we had hid our gold, in which, however, they found themselves deceived.

But I had here another affair upon my hands which was near costing me dear. My servant had been taken from me and left at Mazna, to be sold to the Arabs. Being advertised by him of the danger he was in, I laid claim to him, without knowing the difficulties which this way of proceeding would bring upon me. The governor sent me word that my servant should be restored to me upon payment of sixty piastres; and being answered by me that I had not a penny for myself, and therefore could not pay sixty piastres to redeem my servant, he informed me by a renegade Jew, who negotiated the whole affair, that either I must produce the money or receive a hundred blows of the battoon. Knowing that those orders are without appeal, and always punctually executed, I prepared myself to receive the correction I was threatened with, but unexpectedly found the people so charitable as to lend me the money. By several other threats of the same kind they drew from us about six hundred crowns.

On the 24th of June we embarked in two galleys for Suaquem, where the bassa resided. His brother, who was his deputy at Mazna, made us promise before we went that we would not mention the money he had squeezed from us. The season was not very proper for sailing, and our provisions were but short. In a little time we began to feel the want of better stores, and thought ourselves happy in meeting with a gelve, which, though small, was a much better sailer than our vessel, in which I was sent to Suaquem to procure camels and provisions. I was not much at my ease, alone among six Mahometans, and could not help apprehending that some zealous pilgrim of Mecca might lay hold on this opportunity, in the heat of his devotion, of sacrificing me to his prophet.

These apprehensions were without ground. I contracted an acquaintance, which was soon improved into a friendship, with these people; they offered me part of their provisions, and I gave them some of mine. As we were in a place abounding with oysters—some of which were large and good to eat, others more smooth and shining, in which pearls are found—they gave me some of those they gathered; but whether it happened by trifling our time away in oyster-catching, or whether the wind was not favourable, we came to Suaquem later than the vessel I had left, in which were seven of my companions.

As they had first landed, they had suffered the first transports of the bassa's passion, who was a violent, tyrannical man, and would have killed his own brother for the least advantage—a temper which made him fly into the utmost rage at seeing us poor, tattered, and almost naked; he treated us with the most opprobrious language, and threatened to cut off our heads. We comforted ourselves in this condition, hoping that all our sufferings would end in shedding our blood for the name of Jesus Christ. We knew that the bassa had often made a public declaration before our arrival that he should die contented if he could have the pleasure of killing us all with his own hand. This violent resolution was not lasting; his zeal gave way to his avarice, and he could not think of losing so large a sum as he knew he might expect for our ransom: he therefore sent us word that it was in our choice either to die, or to pay him thirty thousand crowns, and demanded to know our determination.

We knew that his ardent thirst of our blood was now cold, that time and calm reflection and the advice of his friends had all conspired to bring him to a milder temper, and therefore willingly began to treat with him. I told the messenger, being deputed by the rest to manage the affair, that he could not but observe the wretched condition we were in, that we had neither money nor revenues, that what little we had was already taken from us, and that therefore all we could promise was to set a collection on foot, not much doubting but that our brethren would afford us such assistance as might enable us to make him a handsome present according to custom.

This answer was not at all agreeable to the bassa, who returned an answer that he would be satisfied with twenty thousand crowns, provided we paid them on the spot, or gave him good securities for the payment. To this we could only repeat what we had said before: he then proposed to abate five thousand of his last demand, assuring us that unless we came to some agreement, there was no torment so cruel but we should suffer it, and talked of nothing but impaling and flaying us alive; the terror of these threatenings was much increased by his domestics, who told us of many of his cruelties. This is certain, that some time before, he had used some poor pagan merchants in that manner, and had caused the executioner to begin to flay them, when some Brahmin, touched with compassion, generously contributed the sum demanded for their ransom. We had no reason to hope for so much kindness, and, having nothing of our own, could promise no certain sum.

At length some of his favourites whom he most confided in, knowing his cruelty and our inability to pay what he demanded, and apprehending that, if he should put us to the death he threatened, they should soon see the fleets of Portugal in the Red Sea, laying their towns in ashes to revenge it, endeavoured to soften his passion and preserve our lives, offering to advance the sum we should agree for, without any other security than our words. By this assistance, after many interviews with the bassa's agents, we agreed to pay four thousand three hundred crowns, which were accepted on condition that they should be paid down, and we should go on board within two hours: but, changing his resolution on a sudden, he sent us word by his treasurer that two of the most considerable among us should stay behind for security, while the rest went to procure the money they promised. They kept the patriarch and two more fathers, one of which was above fourscore years old, in whose place I chose to remain prisoner, and represented to the bassa that, being worn out with age, he perhaps might die in his hands, which would lose the part of the ransom which was due on his account; that therefore it would be better to choose a younger in his place, offering to stay myself with him, that the good old man might be set at liberty.

The bassa agreed to another Jesuit, and it pleased Heaven that the lot fell upon Father Francis Marquez. I imagined that I might with the same ease get the patriarch out of his hand, but no sooner had I begun to speak but the anger flashed in his eyes, and his look was sufficient to make me stop and despair of success. We parted immediately, leaving the patriarch and two fathers in prison, whom we embraced with tears, and went to take up our lodging on board the vessel.

CHAPTER XV

Their treatment on board the vessel. Their reception at Diou. The author applies to the viceroy for assistance, but without success; he is sent to solicit in Europe.

Our condition here was not much better than that of the illustrious captives whom we left behind. We were in an Arabian ship, with a crew of pilgrims of Mecca, with whom it was a point of religion to insult us. We were lodged upon the deck, exposed to all the injuries of the weather, nor was there the meanest workman or sailor who did not either kick or strike us. When we went first on board, I perceived a humour in my finger, which I neglected at first, till it spread over my hand and swelled up my arm, afflicting me with the most horrid torture. There was neither surgeon nor medicines to be had, nor could I procure anything to ease my pain but a little oil, with which I anointed my arm, and in time found some relief. The weather was very bad, and the wind almost always against us, and, to increase our perplexity, the whole crew, though Moors, were in the greatest apprehension of meeting any of those vessels which the Turks maintain in the strait of Babelmandel; the ground of their fear was that the captain had neglected the last year to touch at Moca, though he had promised. Thus we were in danger of falling into a captivity perhaps more severe than that we had just escaped from. While we were wholly engaged with these apprehensions, we discovered a Turkish ship and galley were come upon us. It was almost calm—at least, there was not wind enough to give us any prospect of escaping—so that when the galley came up to us, we thought ourselves lost without remedy, and had probably fallen into their hands had not a breeze sprung up just in the instant of danger, which carried us down the channel between the mainland and the isle of Babelmandel. I have already said that this passage is difficult and dangerous, which, nevertheless, we passed in the night, without knowing what course we held, and were transported at finding ourselves next morning out of the Red Sea and half a league from Babelmandel. The currents are here so violent that they carried us against our will to Cape Guardafui, where we sent our boats ashore for fresh water, which we began to be in great want of. The captain refused to give us any when we desired some, and treated us with great insolence, till, coming near the land, I spoke to him in a tone more lofty and resolute than I had ever done, and gave him to understand that when he touched at Diou he might have occasion for our interest. This had some effect upon him, and procured us a greater degree of civility than we had met with before.

At length after forty days' sailing we landed at Diou, where we were met by the whole city, it being reported that the patriarch was one of our number; for there was not a gentleman who was not impatient to have the pleasure of beholding that good man, now made famous by his labours and sufferings. It is not in my power to represent the different passions they were affected with at seeing us pale, meagre, without clothes—in a word, almost naked and almost dead with fatigue and ill-usage. They could not behold us in that miserable condition without reflecting on the hardships we had undergone, and our brethren then underwent, in Suaquem and Abyssinia. Amidst their thanks to God for our deliverance, they could not help lamenting the condition of the patriarch and the other missionaries who were in chains, or, at least, in the hands of professed enemies to our holy religion. All this did not hinder them from testifying in the most obliging manner their joy for our deliverance, and paying such honours as surprised the Moors, and made them repent in a moment of the ill-treatment they had shown us on board. One who had discovered somewhat more humanity than the rest thought himself sufficiently honoured when I took him by the hand and presented him to the chief officer of the custom house, who promised to do all the favours that were in his power.

When we passed by in sight of the fort, they gave us three salutes with their cannon, an honour only paid to generals. The chief men of the city, who waited for us on the shore, accompanied us through a crowd of people, whom curiosity had drawn from all parts of our college. Though our place of residence at Diou is one of the most beautiful in all the Indies, we stayed there only a few days, and as soon as we had recovered our fatigues went on board the ships that were appointed to convoy the northern fleet. I was in the admiral's. We arrived at Goa in some vessels bound for Camberia: here we lost a good old Abyssin convert, a man much valued in his order, and who was actually prior of his convent when he left Abyssinia, choosing rather to forsake all for religion than to leave the way of salvation, which God had so mercifully favoured him with the knowledge of.

We continued our voyage, and almost without stopping sailed by Surate and Damam, where the rector of the college came to see us, but so sea-sick that the interview was without any satisfaction on either side. Then landing at Bazaim we were received by our fathers with their accustomed charity, and nothing was thought of but how to put the unpleasing remembrance of our past labours out of our minds. Finding here an order of the Father Provineta to forbid those who returned from the missions to go any farther, it was thought necessary to send an agent to Goa with an account of the revolutions that had happened in Abyssinia and of the imprisonment of the patriarch. For this commission I was made choice of; and, I know not by what hidden degree of Providence, almost all affairs, whatever the success of them was, were transacted by me. All the coasts were beset by Dutch cruisers, which made it difficult to sail without running the hazard of being taken. I went therefore by land from Bazaim to Tana, where we had another college, and from thence to our house of Chaul. Here I hired a narrow light vessel, and, placing eighteen oars on a side, went close by the shore from Chaul to Goa, almost eighty leagues. We were often in danger of being taken, and particularly when we touched at Dabal, where a cruiser blocked up one of the channels through which ships usually sail; but our vessel requiring no great depth of water, and the sea running high, we went through the little channel, and fortunately escaped the cruiser. Though we were yet far from Goa, we expected to arrive there on the next morning, and rowed forward with all the diligence we could. The sea was calm and delightful, and our minds were at ease, for we imagined ourselves past danger; but soon found we had flattered ourselves too soon with security, for we came within sight of several barks of Malabar, which had been hid behind a point of land which we were going to double. Here we had been inevitably taken had not a man called to us from the shore and informed us that among those fishing-boats there, some crusiers would make us a prize. We rewarded our kind informer for the service he had done us, and lay by till night came to shelter us from our enemies. Then putting out our oars we landed at Goa next morning about ten, and were received at our college. It being there a festival day, each had something extraordinary allowed him; the choicest part of our entertainments was two pilchers, which were admired because they came from Portugal.

The quiet I began to enjoy did not make me lose the remembrance of my brethren whom I had left languishing among the rocks of Abyssinia, or groaning in the prisons of Suaquem, whom since I could not set at liberty without the viceroy's assistance, I went to implore it, and did not fail to make use of every motive which could have any influence.

I described in the most pathetic manner I could the miserable state to which the Catholic religion was reduced in a country where it had lately flourished so much by the labours of the Portuguese; I gave him in the strongest terms a representation of all that we had suffered since the death of Sultan Segued, how we had been driven out of Abyssinia, how many times they had attempted to take away our lives, in what manner we had been betrayed and given up to the Turks, the menaces we had been terrified with, the insults we had endured; I laid before him the danger the patriarch was in of being either impaled or flayed alive; the cruelty, insolence and avarice of the Bassa of Suaquem, and the persecution that the Catholics suffered in Fthiopia. I exhorted, I implored him by everything I thought might move him, to make some attempt for the preservation of those who had voluntarily sacrificed their lives for the sake of God. I made it appear with how much ease the Turks might be driven out of the Red Sea, and the Portuguese enjoy all the trade of those countries. I informed him of the navigation of that sea, and the situation of its ports; told him which it would be necessary to make ourselves masters of first, that we might upon any unfortunate encounter retreat to them. I cannot deny that some degree of resentment might appear in my discourse; for, though revenge be prohibited to Christians, I should not have been displeased to have had the Bassa of Suaquem and his brother in my hands, that I might have reproached them with the ill-treatment we had met with from them. This was the reason of my advising to make the first attack upon Mazna, to drive the Turks from thence, to build a citadel, and garrison it with Portuguese.

The viceroy listened with great attention to all I had to say, gave me a long audience, and asked me many questions. He was well pleased with the design of sending a fleet into that sea, and, to give a greater reputation to the enterprise, proposed making his son commander-in-chief, but could by no means be brought to think of fixing garrisons and building fortresses there; all he intended was to plunder all they could, and lay the towns in ashes.

I left no art of persuasion untried to convince him that such a resolution would injure the interests of Christianity, that to enter the Red Sea only to ravage the coasts would so enrage the Turks that they would certainly massacre all the Christian captives, and for ever shut the passage into Abyssinia, and hinder all communication with that empire. It was my opinion that the Portuguese should first establish themselves at Mazna, and that a hundred of them would be sufficient to keep the fort that should be built. He made an offer of only fifty, and proposed that we should collect those few Portuguese who were scattered over Abyssinia. These measures I could not approve.

At length, when it appeared that the viceroy had neither forces nor authority sufficient for this undertaking, it was agreed that I should go immediately into Europe, and represent at Rome and Madrid the miserable condition of the missions of Abyssinia. The viceroy promised that if I could procure any assistance, he would command in person the fleet and forces raised for the expedition, assuring that he thought he could not employ his life better than in a war so holy, and of so great an importance, to the propagation of the Catholic faith.

Encouraged by this discourse of the viceroy, I immediately prepared myself for a voyage to Lisbon, not doubting to obtain upon the least solicitation everything that was necessary to re-establish our mission.

Never had any man a voyage so troublesome as mine, or interrupted with such variety of unhappy accidents; I was shipwrecked on the coast of Natal, I was taken by the Hollanders, and it is not easy to mention the danger which I was exposed to both by land and sea before I arrived at Portugal.